THIRTEEN MONTHS OF SUNSHINE

PEACE CORPS ADVENTURES IN ETHIOPIA: 1962-1964

BY

PATRICIA SUMMERS-PARISH

PublishAmerica
Baltimore

For Niece Mary, Enjoy! Your Aunt Pat Parish

First printing

ISBN: 1-60813-540-3
PUBLISHED BY PUBLISHAMERICA, LLLP
www.publishamerica.com
Baltimore

Printed in the United States of America

TABLE OF CONTENTS

*Throughout this book I spell the capital "Addis *Abeba.*" "Addis" means "new" and "Abeba" means "flower." "Ababa" means father. Since the capital city, Addis Abeba, was to be the "New Flower" of Ethiopia, traditional Western spellings of the capital city appear to be incorrect.

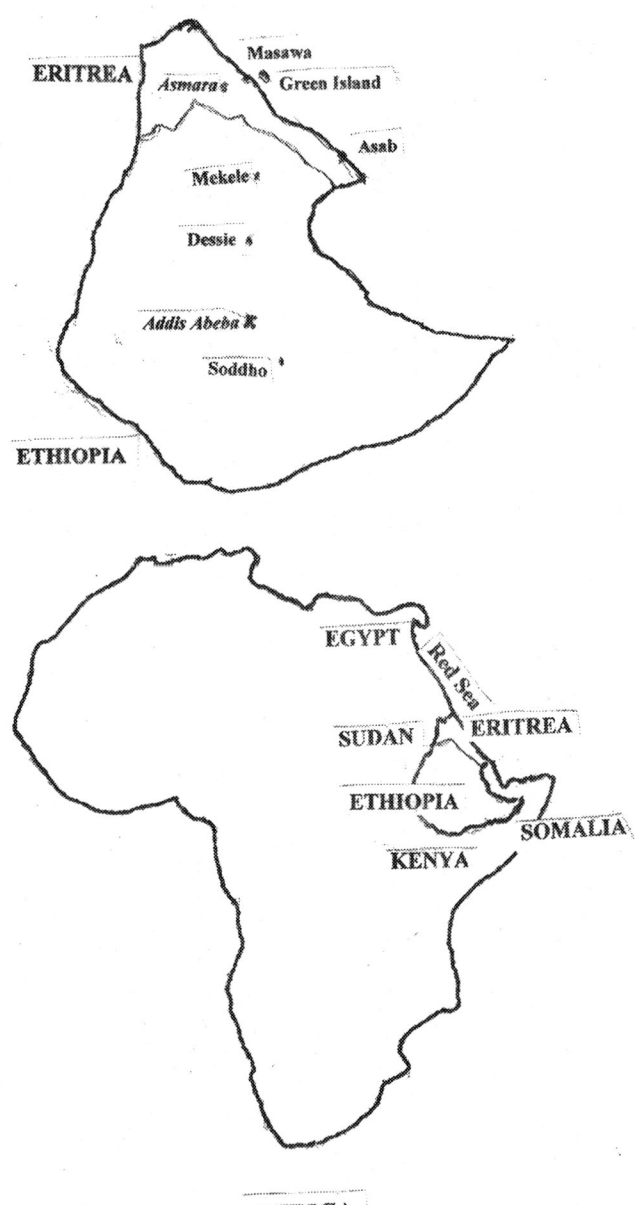

ERITREA

Masawa

Asmara *

Green Island

Asab

Mekele *

Dessie *

Addis Abeba *

Soddho

ETHIOPIA

EGYPT

Red Sea

SUDAN

ERITREA

ETHIOPIA

SOMALIA

KENYA

AFRICA

PROLOGUE

While my husband, whom I met in the Peace Corps back in the early 60's, struggled through three years of surgeries, chemotherapy and radiation, I sat near him reading and reminiscing over our enjoyable and adventuresome past. I was drawn to a drawer in our home where I had placed several large manila folders filled with over 170 letters I had written to my mother during my Peace Corps service in Ethiopia. Before her passing, she had neatly arranged the aerograms, cards and letters in chronological order, numbering each accordingly.

The sixties held many parallels to the present. In the late fifties and early sixties, many Americans read William Lederer's book *The Ugly American*, in which he scathingly wrote of his countrymen who traveled abroad as being arrogant, rude, and demanding. People of high rank and the average indigenous inhabitant of numerous places around the world found visitors from the United States expected everyone to cater to their every wish and to provide them with preferential treatment just because they were U. S. citizens. With the investment in businesses abroad by American entrepreneurs and with many military bases on foreign soil, American families followed these business investments while others moved to the locations of military assignments. Most chose to live on American compounds, which were like little pieces of the U. S. in the middle of Ethiopia, India, Germany, the Philippines, etc. When leaving the compound or military base too many American citizens flaunted their U. S. affiliation, ignored customs of the country, and/or were loud and obnoxious. The build up of these negative impressions led to the common use of the term "the ugly American."

In the sixties we were involved in a highly unpopular war in Viet Nam. Today, much of the world once again looks negatively on the preemptive war in Iraq begun under President Bush. They see the U. S. as a war-mongering nation attempting to turn Iraq into a democracy. Most of the world does not see a connection between this Middle Eastern country and the terrorism of the September 11, 2001 attack on the Twin Towers in New York City, the Pentagon and the downed plane in Pennsylvania. The vast majority of nations were with the U. S. immediately after this disaster when the world saw that thousands of American lives were lost in these acts of terrorism. However, as the Iraq War was prolonged, even after the capture and death of Saddam Hussein, countries have come to look at us as a militant aggressor nation. Once again many view us as "the ugly American."

John F. Kennedy changed the face of the "ugly American" by instituting the Peace Corps. He sought a group of college graduates and older, experienced professionals who would live in towns, villages and rural areas of numerous emerging countries around the globe. This "corps" of people would live in huts and homes typical of each country. They would live within and off the economy of the country of assignment. They were to be a people-to-people program with the intent of endearing the United States, through the Peace Corps, as a dedicated group of educators and encouragers. Most of the early volunteers to the program were filled with altruism and eager to make a difference in the lives of people who had little knowledge of how to use the resources on hand; how to be healthier, more productive, and better educated citizens of their own nations. As volunteers, we had a big task ahead. Many of us went with a great amount of enthusiasm and wanted the people of the world to have a better opinion of our country. We learned much about the people, culture and country of assignment. We learned much about the United States as seen from abroad. We learned much about ourselves.

I hope these excerpts written from the letters I wrote to my mom while I was serving in Ethiopia, help you to understand the Peace Corps experience in a new way and find delight in this country of "13 Months of Sunshine."

ACKNOWLEDGMENTS

This book would not be possible if my mother had not numbered and compiled all the letters written to her during my two years spent in Ethiopia as a Peace Corps teacher. I dedicate this undertaking to her memory.

My husband encouraged me to "do something" with the letters. He enjoyed going through boxes of photos selecting appropriate ones for each chapter. J. B. Morgan suggested I join a writing class to get input for various chapters. Thanks go to her and the members of the class who encouraged me to continue writing about my Peace Corps experiences. Belay Gebre kept finding photos that applied to parts of the book and he deserves thanks also. I am grateful to Ann Dunham for reading over my manuscript in great detail and making numerous suggestions. Marty Gelband was incredible at instructing and assisting me over the phone with computer help. There were many pots of soup and sandwiches made by my husband so I could keep typing.

Most important, of course, was the creation of the Peace Corps by President John F. Kennedy who so eloquently called on people to "...not ask what your county can do for you, rather what you can do for your country." Creating this program to respond to the needs of developing nations, recruiting people to fulfill those needs, training the volunteers, monitoring their well-being while abroad, took logistical expertise. With Sargent Shriver as the first Director of the Peace Corp, the program was underway. I am grateful for the direction and leadership he provided as ordinary Americans were given the opportunity to work and share skills with people in totally different cultures. Hopefully we helped people in many parts of the world to learn positive aspects of America and hopefully we removed some of the stigma of "The Ugly American."

Being a part of this great adventure in American diplomacy changed my life in numerous ways and I feel most fortunate to have served as a Peace Corps Volunteer.

With the 50th anniversary of the Peace Corps approaching in 2010 this book provides a look-back to the early days of its inception.

CHAPTER 1
A DREAM OF AFRICA

From the time I was in fourth grade, I had a love affair with Africa. The enormity of this continent boggled my young mind. From that time on, I read voraciously of the vast plains stretching across level highlands, the immense deserts, savannas dotted with their umbrella-like acacia trees, mysteriously dark rainforests, towering mountains with snow crowning the peaks, and torrential waterfalls. Riding on elephants, swinging on vines that dangled like thick ropes from gigantic trees, training a chimpanzee for a companion, and championing needy tribesmen were some of the fantasies that danced through my impressionable, young mind like the proverbial sugar plums at Christmas time. Of course, watching *Tarzan* movies may have sparked some of my youthful ardor.

Coming from a family of nine children, with my dad a factory laborer, who struggled to care for his family, I found delight in living out my fantasies in the wild imaginations of my mind. Our household was filled with patched, but clean, hand-me-down clothes. We could only afford potatoes for breakfast, lunch and dinner. I knew my loving parents would never be able to provide for the luxury of journeys to exotic places. Therefore, piles of books from the public library assisted my vivid dreams of travel and made my hopes soar to realms far beyond the Milwaukee ghetto we called home. Being the only white girl in many of my junior high school classes, I was given special reading lists by some of the white teachers. My black friends seldom indicated resentment about this, however, since I willingly shared my learnings with everyone. My sincere and warm smile came easily, and I felt at home in my surroundings. Nevertheless, books were my constant companion and prized possessions. In my own books, I underlined, wrote notes in margins, argued with authors, and placed exclamation marks at points of interest. My head, heart, and soul were buried in the thoughts, experiences, challenges, joys and sorrows of others. Dear Mom, would even use my absorption with reading as an excuse to my sisters to overlook my lack of help at meal clean-up times.

As my older brothers and sisters left home to form their own families, more responsibility was placed on me. Dad's sudden, unexpected death, left me alone with my mom and younger brother. Mom's health had become very tenuous two years before losing Dad. With his death, I knew we were living off Aid to Dependent Children, so thoughts of traveling to distant areas of the world became the romantic dream of a teenage girl. The immediate tasks of study, house-cleaning, cooking, laundry, and general care-giving were all-consuming. Occasionally I longed to go out on dates like my friends, but I couldn't afford anything but the simplest wardrobe. I had by now convinced myself that my best date was that with a book, whose pages provided joyous hours of escape.

Amazingly, avid reading had paved a road for excelling in all subjects at school, and a number of college scholarships materialized at graduation. I still dreamed of Hemingway's *Green Hills of Africa*, wept as I read Alan Paton's *Cry the Beloved Country*, and *Too Late the Phalarope*. I was thrilled by the various biographies of Albert Schweitzer. However, I was resigned to the fact that all my travel would be vicarious. A teaching credential would be the quickest way to provide for my family.

Shortly after my dad's death, I became a Christian. Through "searching the Scriptures," God gave a new fervor for life and I joined a church. The words of the hymns meant more and more to me. I started to learn the importance of being true, honorable, just, pure, lovely, gracious, excellent, and worthy of praise, as was taught in the New Testament. Youth for Christ impacted me in my last year of high school and Inter-Varsity Christian Fellowship, in College. God was teaching me to be content wherever I was. Missionary biographies began to filter into my reading choices. Was this to be my destiny? The financial arrangements for this type of calling scared me. My faith was too weak.

A part-time job at Fink's Drug Store and later at the First Wisconsin National Bank, and immersion in studies to maintain scholarships, would eventually reward me with my college degree and a teaching credential from the University of Wisconsin-Milwaukee. Africa was still John Wayne in *Hatari* and Peter O'Toole in *Lawrence of Arabia*; Kathryn Hepburn and Humphrey Bogart in *African Queen*, and Ava Gardner in *Snows of Kilimanjaro*. The song "Far Away Places with Strange Sounding Names" made me yearn to travel.

The fifties and sixties were also a time of African upheaval as wars for independence spread like wild-fires across the continent. Movements for Nationhood erupted—Jomo Kenyata in Kenya; Kenneth Kaunda in Zambia; Joseph Kasavuba and Patrice Lumumba in Congo; etc. etc. I hungered to know more, but humorously celebrated Africa's coming of age by purchasing a large carved hippopotamus and naming it "Kasavubu-Lumumba."

As I began my second year of teaching junior high school in Milwaukee, the young John F. Kennedy gave his Presidential inaugural address to the nation. My heart, like many others, was stirred by his request to "…ask not what your country can do for you, but rather what you can do for your country…" The plans for a corps of Americans, young and old, who wished to share our country with needy people of other cultures, began to take shape. When the Peace Corps was announced, I prayed with my mom that somehow, I could respond. An opportunity to travel at government expense and use my teaching skills in a distant area of the world, was being offered. Could mom and my younger brother, who had graduated from high school, manage without me and the income I was now bringing home? Would my married brothers and sisters be able to step into the breech? I loved them all dearly, but would their Republican or Democratic leanings diminish the joy of my choosing to join what some were referring to as "JFK's Peace Corps" or "Kennedy Kids?"

Dear, sweet, wise Mom said, "Your family loves and respects your knowledge and your eagerness to travel. They know how hard you have worked. They'll all come around. Health and money may fade, but the experiences you acquire will remain an integral part of you for as long as you exist. Go, experience your dreams."

Upon completion of an extensive application, a day of examinations, and a physical exam, I received the most exciting phone call of my life. The call was from Harris Wofford, head of the Peace Corps in Africa. He invited me to enter training for the Ethiopia I Project which was to begin training at Georgetown University in Washington, D.C. this summer of 1962!

And so my dream was about to become reality.

CHAPTER 2
WHERE IN THE WORLD IS ETHIOPIA?

After the shock of being invited to join the Peace Corps Ethiopia I Project had worn off, my brain was overflowing with questions. Where *is* Ethiopia? What is the land and climate like? Will I live in a jungle? A desert? What kind of clothing will I need to take along? What is the history of this area? What will the people be like? Zillions of questions tumbled around in my head like clothing in an automatic dryer, bumping against each other and getting hopelessly entangled. I barely knew where to begin, so I turned to my best friends— BOOKS!

Ethiopia is located north of the Equator in East Africa, on a portion known as the "Horn of Africa," I read. The northernmost province of Eritrea borders the Red Sea. The Eritrean cities of Massawa and Assab are ports on the Red Sea. Periodically, Eritrea has separated itself from Ethiopia, leaving the country landlocked. To the west of Ethiopia is the Sudan; to the south is Kenya; and to the east is Somalia—now divided into Djibouti and Somalia. The Great Rift Valley slices through the country from north to south forming high mountains that tower over the Danakil Depression located in the eastern part of the country. This depression forms one of the lowest deserts on earth. Temperatures vary from cold mountains with occasional snow, to temperate highland plateaus, to extremely hot deserts. The seaports have reported some of the hottest temperatures known. Apparently no real jungles are in Ethiopia. I won't find Tarzan here! The capital is Addis Abeba, which means "New Flower" and it is located almost in the middle of the country at an elevation of about 8000 feet. The city sprawls over a vast area of a high plateau. Rolling mountain ranges surround the plateau in the distance.

Ethiopians was called "Abyssinia" or the "Land of the Queen of Sheba." Most Ethiopian believed they were descendants of King Solomon, son of David in the *Bible*, and the Queen of Sheba. A number of Biblical references added strength to this belief. The Coptic Church in Ethiopia believed the Ark of the Covenant, depicted in Jewish writings and in the "Old Testament," resided in the Northern Ethiopian city of Aksum. King Solomon had given the Ark to the son he had had with Sheba. Menelik was the son's name. A tribe, the Falashas, who held to strict Jewish traditions, also inhabited one of the Ethiopian mountain strongholds for centuries. They gave further strength to the relationship of Ethiopia with Israel. The Falashas believed themselves to be the "Lost Tribe of Israel," or the Black Jews of Africa. The Solomon and Sheba story was exciting to me, for here was some Biblical history with which I was familiar.

The last Emperor of Ethiopia, Haile Selassie I, King of Kings, Conquering Lion of the Tribe of Judah, claimed direct lineage to Menelik I. Would I get to meet the Emperor of this country? [The Emperor was assassinated in 1982. He had ruled for fifty-seven years.]

Ethiopia had always been independent of European domination, except for a brief occupation by Italy during World War II.

The primary language, Amharic, is spoken only in Ethiopia. It has its own script of over two hundred symbols for letters and numbers. Other tribal languages abound. Some English, French, Italian, and Arabic can be heard throughout the land. A new language with a new script, only used in Ethiopia, would be a challenge, indeed.

With only limited knowledge of the country to which I was going, I was ready to be immersed, saturated, and filled to the brim with everything Ethiopia that Georgetown University training could place before me. Bring it on!

CHAPTER 3
GEORGETOWN UNIVERSITY
PEACE CORPS TRAINING

Dormitories at Georgetown U. were commodious, but without air-conditioning. We sweltered in the heat of a Washington, D.C. summer in 1962!

A typical day began with physical education at 5:30 A.M., before the sun make steam rise from the grass. We ran and performed calisthenics daily. By 7:00 A.M. we had showered and changed for breakfast. Eight in the morning found us in language laboratories, using earphones to become familiar with the sounds of Amharic. Our voluminous language manual guided us through most commonly used phrases, while recording machines picked up our pronunciations and played them back to us. We met in small groups for practicing Amharic orally with Ethiopian instructors, and attended classes where we practiced writing and deciphering the written script. In addition, we learned about geography, history, culture, customs, tribal groupings, taboos, and politics. Health issues were extensively and intensively discussed. The need for boiling and filtering water, careful food preparations, health, and hygiene issues were drummed home. Seminars for teaching our subject matter took up big portions of the day. I would be teaching English as a Second Language and special strategies were part of my instruction. Lunch was sandwiched in around noon. Classes continued after lunch.

Down time or study hall was given before dinner. Dessert frequently had us lining-up after dinner to receive two or three injections to protect and fortify our bodies. By the end of the first month of our two months of training, we all felt like pin-cushions! Georgetown Dental School also gave us complete check-ups, replaced old fillings in our teeth, and pulled all impacted wisdom teeth. There was one weekend when over two hundred PCV's (Peace Corps Volunteers) walked around the campus looking like chipmunks, with ice packs gingerly held to one or both swollen cheeks! Our government certainly wanted to send the healthiest specimens abroad.

Some evenings we heard from experts on various aspects of Ethiopia or foreign policy. Films or slides of the country were shown. All seminars were followed by question/answer sessions. We could also use the language labs or study hall for those so inclined. Others, who were monetarily endowed, enjoyed socializing in the local pubs.

Several evenings weekly we had to report to a gathering place at 10:00 P.M. to board buses for Glen Echo Park in Maryland. Our group of nearly four hundred trainees used the park's swimming facilities after the park was closed to the public. We usually arrived slightly before the park closed and enjoyed the rides, for me it was the roller coaster! In the pools we were given instruction on careful life-saving techniques. By one in the morning, we crashed into our beds, only to report by 5:30 A.M. on the P.E. field for another full day of activities.

Weekends brought some variations. We were entertained at some embassies; we visited museums and national monuments; we saw theatrical productions; we completed a two-day, twenty-five mile hike through the Alleghenies, with only a large piece of blue plastic to wrap ourselves in at night. We looked like some four hundred blue burritos sleeping on the ground!

The highlight of our training program was being presented to President John F. Kennedy in the Rose Garden of the White House! We were the largest group to complete Peace Corps training, and the first to go to Ethiopia.

At the completion of our *two* months of training, we were sent home for *two* weeks to pack enough for *two* years into *two* foot lockers. And I'll bet you thought an overnighter took a lot of planning!

CHAPTER 4
NEW YORK TO ATHENS TO ETHIOPIA

A red-eye flight to New York's Idlewild Airport, arriving at 1:00 A.M. on September 6, 1962, began my two year adventure! My sister, Marilyn, had driven from Long Island to the beautiful, new TWA terminal to keep me company from 1:00 A.M. to 7:30 A.M. It was so good to have a family member here to bid me farewell. I introduced her to some of the PCV's when they arrived, and we all breakfasted together. Marilyn hugged me tightly, as our group was called, and we said our farewells.

Excitement was building up as our passports and health cards were distributed to us. Was this really happening? Passports meant foreign soil. Would I be able to discern that which was good, just, kind, humble, generous, excellent, worthy of praise no matter where I was? Would I allow God to help me make a difference? I silently asked God to make me a blessing to my new Peace Corps friends and to the many Ethiopians I was soon to meet. I was calmed.

At 10:00 A.M. we boarded our huge, trans-oceanic super-jet, my first big plane! It was luxuriously comfortable as we crossed the Atlantic, flew over France, and stopped to re-fuel in Rome at 11:30 at night. We all rushed to buy postcards. I squished a detailed itinerary into the minute space allowed for writing, and mailed the missal to Mom. Our half hour lay-over flew by faster than our super-jet, and we were soon boarding for a brief flight to Athens, Greece, the city built by Pericles in ancient times with the wonder of the Acropolis and the Parthenon—AND WE HAD A WHOLE DAY TO SEE THIS ANCIENT CITY!

After arriving in Athens and having our passports checked, we were taken by bus to clean, modern hotels with private baths. Lonia, an African-American girl, Cindy Tse, a Chinese-American girl, and I roomed together. Our room on the seventh floor of the hotel, had a balcony that over-looked Athens. Beyond the slate-topped roofs of the city, we could view dusty-brown rolling hills in the distance. Perched on one hill we could see what appeared to be an old white monastery. Since we had slept a bit on the plane, we needed only a few hours of sleep to refresh ourselves before exploring this ancient city.

We breakfasted at the hotel. It was interesting ordering and asking directions, since we knew no Greek and the people could not speak English. I remembered a few words of French and that helped us get by.

As we started on our hike to the Acropolis, we met some of the Peace Corps fellows. We had to walk miles through the business section of town where both sidewalks and streets alike, teamed with hordes of people rushing every which way. It was hundreds of times worse that the day before Christmas at Gimbel's Department Store! Cars honked incessantly at people to get out of their way. The cars kept coming if people didn't move! People and cars constantly brushed, bumped, or just missed each other! In many places stall-like shops came right up to the road, and wares were on display every which place. People constantly smiled or called to us to try or buy their merchandise.

Along the way, we passed many walled-in places that contained the ruins of ancient edifices. We stopped to see some, but our destination was the Acropolis. We climbed the steps to the top of this ancient hill and stood in awe of the impressive ruins—the Parthenon, the Temple of Athena, the Amphitheater, and more architectural wonders, all strikingly beautiful in the intense rays of the Grecian sun. The views of the city were also spectacular from the Acropolis. We spent hours exploring. As we descended, we found a refreshing ice cream stand at the base of the Acropolis. We enjoyed the treat while we "talked" with some Greeks and rested in some welcome shade. After all the walking, we braved taking a taxi back to our hotel for lunch. The treacherously careening car seemed to brush against every vehicle, large or small, as it darted along in quick starts and equally quick stops. It zoomed around other vehicles and squeezed into impossible openings between carts and cars. Drivers and passengers in other cars shook fists and shouted obscenities in Greek at our driver. Swarming pedestrians appeared to bounce out of our way. We hung onto each other inside the vehicle as we were thrown around. If we survived this ride, we could survive anything! In retrospect, it was amusing.

The afternoon was spent visiting more museums, shopping and spending a few drachmas.

It was now time to find the Ethiopian Airways office for a ride back to the airport. Our bus ride to the airline's office was also eventful. In asking directions, we had to pantomime a plane, by pointing and gesticulating our requests! We must have looked ridiculous, but apparently we were effective.

At 10:00 P.M. we boarded Ethiopian Airways DC-6's for our flight across the Mediterranean Sea, across Egypt and the Sudan, and finally into Ethiopia!

CHAPTER 5
ADDIS ABEBA, ETHIOPIA

After an all night flight, we arrived in the capital at eight in the morning. The airport was packed with Ethiopians and Americans all there to welcome us. We felt like celebrities as we passed through the reception lines, shaking hands with dozens of people, while photographers snapped pictures constantly.

Finally, we were put on buses and driven through the streets of Addis to the University College of Addis Abeba. Here we were assigned rooms in the dormitories, and our luggage was brought to us. The dormitories were very simple but comfortable. I had a metal bed with a thin mattress and a "rock" pillow, sheets, and two blankets, both of which we needed for the cold nights at an altitude of eight thousand feet! There was also a desk, electric lamp, and a small closet.

We were given the morning and afternoon for sleeping and settling in. To be in a prone position after sleeping in seats for the long trip, was especially welcome. The bathroom smells took some adjustment; likewise, the cold showers. All in all, I thought we had it pretty good!

Schedules for our two weeks' orientation in Addis were distributed that evening. We were to be taken on numerous tours of the city and its surroundings, visiting Koka Dam, Wonji Sugar Plantation and Factory, Coptic churches with their Byzantine influences, and market places. The culminating activity was to be our presentation to Emperor Haile Selassie at Jubilee Palace. We were also given our first paycheck—seventy five dollars Ethiopian, which is approximately thirty dollars American.

With money in our pockets came our first foray into the main shopping center in this capital. Souks, lean-to's, open front shops and buildings were squashed together barely a few feet from the roadway. Clothing, food, pots, baskets, and wares of all kind were displayed in every available space. There were a few places that actually appeared to be what we were used to as stores—buildings with glass windows, a small display and clean interior. People sat, stood, walked, leaned everywhere, appearing to be extremely busy doing nothing. Scantily and shabbily clad children seemed to ooze out of every crevasse, smiling at us and calling, "Hey, Ferengi (foreigner)." Some held out a hand or tried to sell us gum for a quarter. A variety of clothing garbed the shoppers: white blanket-like wrappings from head to toe with only eyes peeking out; long, white Ethiopian dresses with shawls wound around shoulders; veiled Muslim women; turbaned men; women in colorful saris; and even some modern Western wear.

Bartering was another new experience, and I'm sure we spent too much on articles purchased. However, our excursion gave us ample opportunity to use our Amharic, a feat which amazed and never ceased to bring a grin to the faces of the Ethiopians.

Strange, and difficult-to-identify smells, assaulted our noses. Diesel fumes, unwashed bodies, cooking oils, animal and human waste, and some incense were odors that intermingled freely. This will definitely take some olfactory adjusting.

Many PCV's complained about the food at the University dining hall. In an attempt to Americanize the food, cooking oil was liberally used and food was very greasy. The dishes were not always clean. However, our biggest problem was water. We were not supposed to drink the water in Ethiopia without boiling and filtering it, and since we had no facilities for this, we were out of luck. I could hardly wait to get on our own so as to take care of all our necessary sanitation and health measures. We did find some bottled water we could buy.

On one of our days we visited Haile Selassie I University, which used to be one of the Emperor's old palaces. We were hosted to tea and a reception. The palace was set back at the end of a line of palm and banana trees. Exotic flower gardens surrounded the building, as they do every place of importance. Young boys served as gardeners, cutting the lawns by hand with sickles. Beautiful roses, calla lilies, and poinsettias flourished. The building itself looked like a Bermuda summer home, as Sommerset Maugham might have described in one of his novels. Brownish-red bamboo awnings covered the windows of a grayish-white stucco house. From the outside it was unimposing. Inside, a thick red carpet led to a long reception hall. Here the Minister of Education greeted us. We were escorted upstairs to an elegant ballroom where a glistening chandelier sparkled overhead. Hors d'oevres and petit fours were scarfed down by our hungry horde eager to savor familiar flavors. The ballroom opened unto a terrace at the front of the palace. It looked out over the gardens with a breath-taking backdrop of mountains in every shade of green and purple. The ranges changed color with the movement of the clouds. These same clouds had brought us rain every day since we arrived, but somehow, the sun seemed to find time to come out daily.

The weather, compounded by altitude and rain, had been rather chilly since our arrival. I was glad that I had packed some woolens in my carry-on luggage.

On leaving the reception, we passed one of the zoos where some of the Emperor's lions and cheetahs were kept. He had around fifty of them. At a later date we visited the zoo and found the animals here to be better fed than many of the Emperor's subjects, a rather dismaying fact—a fact that could even breed revolution. On another occasion, I even went into a cheetah cage and petted the well-fed beast, as I pondered the problems facing the beggars seen on the streets. We were told not to give to beggars.

One evening, a group of us went to the Italian Club in town to play ping-pong, chess, checkers, and cards. The evening ended pleasantly, except for the taxi ride home. Somehow, I would have to get used to riding on the opposite side of the street. There are no rules of the road, so cars fly down streets and zip through intersections, that have no stop signs nor directional lights! Brakes are given a real workout! Several of us needed umbrellas, boots, wash pails and hangers. Another marketing jaunt with a few jolts was in store.

CHAPTER 6
NEW FRIENDS, FELLOWSHIP,
AND AN EMPEROR

I had just finished a cold shower and hair wash at our dorm, when one of the girls asked if I would lead some of them in devotions. Because of our hectic schedule, we had not been able to visit any church service yet, so ten girls met in my room. I led in a devotion on "Psalm 19," and we sang some hymns. One of the Peace Corps girls asked God to bless our stay in Ethiopia, and to provide us all with health, protection, friends, and fellowship.

Another bus-escorted-trip to the market place began with a drive all over the business section of Addis and then down into the Marketo. This market place was akin to the ones seen in movies about this area of the world. It stretched on forever. Here were thousands of covered stalls and lean-to's stretching as far as the eye could see. Also there were men and women squatting on blankets with their wares in baskets or spread out before them. People, robed in Middle Eastern garb, called and sang out their wares in all kinds of strange dialects and tones. Lonia, Cindy and I disembarked with an Ethiopian, who offered to be our guide.

Obtaining umbrellas, hangers, and pails kept us so involved that the buses had departed without us. When our guide, Girma Stephanos, asked about the buses, it seemed as if half of the market place wanted to find out what was being asked. Veiled women, turbaned and nonturbaned men, dark-eyed children peering from behind skirts, goats and cows, ALL crowded around us—some to give information;

most out of curiosity. We finally discovered in which direction the buses had gone, and Ato Girma (Ato being a title like Mr.) called for a taxi. To call for a taxi in Ethiopia in a crowded place, meant literally that. One stands and shouts, "Taxi!" Even if one isn't in sight, all of a sudden, multiple taxis appear, from every direction! Taxis were nearly running over blankets, people, cows, and goats alike! Two even bumped into each other!

We finally climbed into one of the taxis and were off, precariously dodging through masses of people, some carrying gigantic loads of twigs on their backs, others with enormous baskets on their heads. Also in danger were mule pack trains, and busy Ethiopian shoppers! How we arrived at our bus's new location with no injury to human, beast, or vehicle, remains a mystery. Some protective angel, with a sense of humor, must have heard the requests in our devotions this morning.

Ethiopians were always generous in offering us rides in their own cars. The Minister of Education took us to our dorms in his Mercedes after one day of programs held several miles outside of the city. On the way home, he bought seven, live chickens whose legs were tied together, and put them in the trunk of the car. We could hear them squawking all the way to Addis, and felt sympathy for them, until we felt their companions—copious amounts of FLEAS that were now visibly jumping and feasting on us! The chickens were for the New Year's dinner celebration in two days.

We had arrived in Ethiopia during "Meskaram," the month heralding the Ethiopian New Year, which this year arrived on September eleventh on our calendar. There are thirteen months on the Ethiopian calendar year—twelve consist of thirty days, and one of six days. There is also a seven year difference in the Ethiopian calendar from the one we use. For instance, we came to Ethiopia in 1962 on our calendar, but it is 1955 on their calendar. Rather confusing, isn't it?

New Year's Eve was pretty eventful. A group of us were planning on a restful dinner at the Chinese restaurant in Addis. Several taxis pulled up in front of our dorm, and PCV's piled into them. Before we knew it, the taxis had pulled away, leaving Lonia, Cindy, John Bigelow and me still there. Immediately, a little car pulled up and offered to drive us to where we all wanted to go. Since this was typical here, and since there was a fellow along, we accepted. On our way to the restaurant, we discovered that our Ethiopian driver was a representative for the Bank of Ethiopia and had just returned from Kenya. He insisted that we all join his party at a big restaurant for the New Year's Eve celebration as his guests.

"This will probably be your only time in Addis on New Year's Eve," he persuaded. He drove us back to our dorms to dress up. The holiday is apparently celebrated pretty much like in the States. However, as we rode to the party, we saw people festively building fires in front of their homes, and young people carrying sparklers and flares. There were big bonfires in some locations. Such bright warm greetings were for welcoming the New Year, we were told. Our host had already picked up and transported more of his friends: another banker, the headmaster of the school in Massawa, a pilot for Ethiopian Airways, and a municipal officer. The restaurant was very huge and exclusive. An Ethiopian band played both rock and roll as well as Ethiopian music. A young Ethiopian, looking and sounding like Elvis Presley, made a great hit with the audience. An American, who had been introduced as the one in charge of training the pilots for Ethiopian Airways, was very cynical and said quietly to me that he disliked Ethiopians. His snobbish behavior and critical words made him appear to have stepped from pages of *The Ugly American*. He was an embarrassment to everything the Peace Corps was hoping to accomplish.

Later in the evening, we were served "injerra and wat," the national dish of Ethiopia. Injerra is a large flat grayish pancake with a pungently sour taste. Wat is an extremely spicey stew. Pieces of injerra are pulled off the rubbery "pancake" with fingers of the right hand, and dipped into the spicy, hot wat, scooping a little up. The right hand is the required hand to do this. The strange flavors with the hot, berbere sauce felt like one was swallowing magma from a volcano! Tears gushed from my eyes, as well as from the other Americans in our group. The Ethiopians thought this was hilarious, and said that we would get used to it during our stay here. American food is very bland in comparison—three cheers for bland food!

New Year's Day was spent visiting homes of Ethiopians. We were divided into groups of two to four for the visits. I went with another PCV whose name escapes me. We were picked up by car. There are surprisingly, a number of cars in Addis Abeba. Most are small like Fiats and Volkswagens. The car stopped at a low gate. Here we had to bend down to get into the yard where sheep could be heard bleating somewhere behind the house, and an occasional moo came from a cow in some direction beyond the house. A few chickens ran across our feet as we stepped over the stones onto steps that led to the small front porch of a rectangular structure. Two doors, like narrow French doors, opened into a small front room. Most of the homes in this area are made of a framework of wood tied together with rope, then filled in with more pieces of wood woven in-between wooden posts. The wood is then filled in with mud and dung and smoothed so that the outside of the walls had the appearance of adobe. Some people can afford to paint the inside and outside of the home. The house we visited was painted yellow in and out.

Most roofs were made of corrugated tin. This became all too apparent as the usual afternoon deluge began. Our conversations were drowned by the thunder of the pouring rain on the metal roof.

The floors of the house were wooden planks covered in cement. Furnishings consisted of chairs with cushions, a table, bookshelves, and a stereo-tape recorder on which Ethiopian music played. A dining area was off the front room. This is where we ate—injerra and wat again! I'm afraid I am not adjusting well to this cuisine. A very solicitous house-boy stood behind us ready to replace anything we had eaten on our dish. I tried to distract our host from my lack of appetite by using as much Amharic as I could remember. The household seemed entertained by this.

After dinner we were driven around the city, stopping to see the scenic beauty which is everywhere. The majestic mountain ranges and rolling hillsides, with rain-spent clouds constantly changing colors and patterns on our surroundings, provided us with breathtaking views. At one stop a group of children came along the road singing and selling flowers. I was given a lovely bouquet while the custom of "caroling" on "Addis Zeman" or New Year's Day, was shared by our host. What generous, hospitable people inhabit our host country!

Another dinner-dance was held that evening by the Ministry of Education at another exclusive restaurant. This time a buffet was laid before us with many recognizable and tasty offerings. Raw meat was offered to us as a delicacy. I smilingly declined the delicacy.

Our visit to Jubilee Palace, Emperor Haile Selassie's residence, was memorable. After being ushered into the foyer, which was guarded by His Imperial Majesty's pet cheetahs, we walked into the long throne room where we all filed past Emperor Hail Selassie I, King of Kings, Conquering Lion of the Tribe of Judah. Although short and slight of stature, his dignity made me feel like I was in the presence of a giant. Each of us was introduced and shook the hand of this historical figurehead. While His Majesty made a short speech to us, his two pet dogs, which were running around his feet, started yapping their heads off. We found it difficult to keep straight faces. However, a glance at the solemn Ethiopians present, quietly warned us to control ourselves. Soon waiters entered with trays of champagne and hors d'ouevres. How awesome it was to think I was standing in the presence of the Emperor of the oldest kingdom in the world!

On Sunday, September sixteenth, I finally was able to get to the Sudan Interior Mission Station! I had called before going, and people were waiting for me at the gate to their compound. After services and Bible class, I was invited to join them for dinner—an American dinner of roast chicken, dressing, mashed potatoes, gravy, cranberry, carrots and peas, and ice cream with raspberries! Joy! Joy! My fellow PCV's, who don't enjoy going to church, don't know what they are missing! In the afternoon we drove over to Bingham Academy, the school for missionary children, where the children put on a program. Here supper was served and we ate with the 108 students. Then we returned to the mission in Addis for the evening service, where I sang a solo, "How Great Thou Art." After the service, tea and cake was served for the two hundred in attendance. Present were Ethiopians, Brits, some Scandinavians, and Americans. Several Americans were U.S. Government Point-4 workers, people who advise Ethiopia with agriculture, education, finance and health. In addition, a few Americans were U.S.A.I.D. personnel. I met many missionaries. When I told them that I would be teaching in Dessie, they told me of their SIM Leprosarium near there. In fact, they immediately wrote to them of my coming, so that the missionaries at Boro Meda Leprosarium could contact me.

I thought to myself, "Thank you, thank you, Lord of my life! You, indeed, have been watching over me! I am being sent to Dessie where there will be people who already know about my arrival! How blessed I am! May I share the joy You bring and be a blessing to others."

CHAPTER 7
ARRIVAL IN DESSIE

Our bus ride from Addis took fourteen hours to cover two hundred and fifty kilometers. The hair-pin turns of this mountainous road, climbing up the escarpment of the Great Rift Valley with drop-offs of 2000 to 3000 feet in places, had me white-knuckling the back of the seat in front of me at times. The deep, cavernous valleys and the towering green and purple mountains, with stretches of high plateaus, both rising from the floor beneath, could hold a dozen Grand Canyons in their great out-stretched arms. A kaleidoscope of colors danced a ballet, as cloud formations leisurely glided above the landscape. Such beauty craved more adequate description than my feeble attempts at such.

The only road that traversed this country from north to south had been built during the World War II Italian occupation which lasted approximately seven years. The bumps and crater-size potholes indicated little maintenance of this narrow, winding, unending road. Groups of round mud huts with grass roofs, called "tukels" by some, but referred to as "sarbets" (grass houses in Amharic), dotted portions of the landscape, especially where a stand of trees could be found. Trees indicated much needed water was nearby. Small villages, with a dozen or so rectangular mud huts, sporadically lined the road. We took rest stops at a few of the villages. At one village eatery, injerra and wat was served along with hot tea or warm Coca Cola—no refrigeration here! Prior to eating, we went to a basin on a stand where soap, a jug of water and a towel were available for washing. Since restrooms were non-existent, we fetched blankets from the bus, went to a nearby field, and took turns holding up the "privacy screen' to relieve ourselves. We shared a roll of toilet paper, soon learning that blankets and toilet paper would go wherever we went!

Our bus, which had climbed over endless circuitous roads to mountain ranges of great heights, finally made a gentle descent over a slight rise. Dessie, my home for the next two years, lay before us. The town sat astride a jutting plateau that held tightly to slopes that slanted upwards to, what looked like, smoothly, rounded mountain tops. In the distance, lofty ridges and towering ranges and verdant green hills rolled on and on as far as the eye could see. Could there possibly be a more beautiful place on earth?

Stately eucalyptus, umbrella-like acacias, candelabra, and false banana trees were everywhere along with a myriad of colorful flowers. Horse drawn gherrys clomped down the streets as did pack-mule trains and donkeys, laden with heavy-looking burdens. Dark-skinned men and women, wrapped in shammas (shawls), many carrying cumbersome loads, threw curious glances at our bus, as did the beggars sitting along the roadside. They looked up at the loaded dusty vehicle and the white faces peering out the windows. Now and then we saw a lepper, a person with rickets, or a man with elephantiasis, a disease causing the person's leg or legs to look like enormous tree trunks. They also stopped along pathways and stared as our bus made its way to the Touring Hotel in town. We saw very few motorized vehicles.

Along the way I noted that a number of the houses were rectangular with tin roofs like the homes we had visited in Addis. Instead of glass window, many appeared to have a type of Venetian blind shutter, which hung open against the walls of the house during the day, but could be pulled closed at night. Many of the structures were almost hidden by trees or flowers.

We were told Dessie was the third largest city in the country and had a population of around eighty thousand. It was so much cleaner than Addis, with fresher air and fewer obnoxious odors. Surpassing everything in sight, was the absolute grandeur of the powerful mountain towering above the town and the endless ranges of hills stretching forever beyond the rest of the village. Since our residences weren't quite ready, we were housed at the Dessie Touring Hotel.

Early morning, sounds of donkeys braying, roosters crowing, cattle lowing, voices calling to each other in Amharic, caused me to jump from my bed and fly to the shutters, throw them back, and greet my first day in Dessie. Verdant green meadows rushed to the slope of a towering mountain, where barefooted people on steep pathways carefully picked their way down to a gravel road already filled with brown-skinned people who were herding cows, goats or sheep. All walked purposefully. Many of the men wore long, grayish-white, wrap-around skirts with shammas thrown around their necks and shoulders. A long stick rested behind the neck, with both hands holding it on either side. Periodically, the stick was used to smack a donkey or cow for keeping it in line. A few of the older men used theirs for walking sticks. There were men in suit coats and jodhpurs, carrying an umbrella for protection from the sun, and riding on donkeys with several barefoot servants running along side. Groups of barefoot women with long, formerly white dresses and carrying water jugs, babies, or a load of washing to take to the river, called greetings to each other. In the opposite direction, came women with huge loads of twigs and kindling tied up in enormous bundles and strapped to their backs and foreheads. Barefooted men, women, and children carrying large, woven baskets, moved in a constant two-way parade of people.

The grounds of the Touring Hotel were being manicured by several cows and goats. A fat mother pig rooted around while her five piglets hungrily squealed behind her. Sheep could be heard in the distance. The smell of breakfast lured our PCV crowd to the dining hall. With stomachs fortified, several of us made the kilometer walk to the piazza, or center of town. Here in a circular arrangement around the outside of the piazza were the Bank of Ethiopia, the Army Barracks (which had been the Fascist headquarters during WW II), the Telecommunications Building, with our local post office, a coffee house (buna bet), a number of Arab shops (souks), and the road that led us up the hill to the school where we would be teaching—Woizero Siheen Timherte Bet.

The only structure, located on a hill higher than the school, was the Coptic Church. It had its own school for instructing youngsters in Amharic script and in church teachings. There was also a mosque in Dessie. Muezzins could be heard singing out five times a day from their minarets to their believers in town.

We were impressed by one very new, two-story building of classrooms as we went through the gates of the school compound. At the top of the hill was an older building with more rooms, and scattered around the other side of this building were additional tin-roofed cubicles. My English as a Second Language (ESL) classes would be held in one of these rooms. School was soon to begin.

We finally moved into our house! My housemates were Carolyn Mulford from Missouri, Jean Bottcher from Pennsylvania, Arwilda Bryant from Texas, Marian Lynch from North Carolina, and Cora Morehead from Washington, D.C. Let me tell you a little about each of them.

The oldest in our house was a beautiful African-American girl, tall and slender, named Cora, She was 28 and from Washington, D.C. her home town where she had taught for several years. She had a M.A. in elementary education and taught all the teacher training courses. Her sense of humor was one developed from living in a large family. She didn't like house work very much but she was so funny about it that it didn't bother any of us. She was a smoker, but very pleasant to be around. Whenever something bothered her, she retreated to her room, but she was always ready and willing to help everyone. Cora carried herself so beautifully; she looked like an African queen.

Carolyn was about 24 and from a little town in Missouri. She graduated from the University of Missouri where she got her Master's

Degree in journalism. She hadn't taught before joining the Peace Corps, and, as a result, has had some discipline problems with her eleventh grade classes. Nevertheless, she was a conscientious teacher, always correcting papers. Her nose was frequently buried in the wonderful array of books sent to us by the Peace Corps in a huge foot-locker. Carolyn was short and stocky. She was quite solemn. She took her work very seriously but was not excited about housekeeping. However, she loved the trips to Boro Meda, as the SIM Leprosarium was called. I think she loved the familiar food we were always served there.

Jean Bottcher was about 23 and a graduate of Cornell University. She appeared to come from a rather cultured family near Pittsburgh. Her parents had given her a tour of Europe as a graduation present. At first Jean struck me as being cold, distant, and selfish. However, I think this was just a cover-up. She liked being alone and often locked herself in her room. She was an avid reader and had subscriptions to *Harpers, The New Yorker* and other magazines that were coming to her here. She was teaching seventh grade English and social studies. At first she seemed unconcerned about anything in the house. However, her family had begun sending her a number of packages containing baking mixes. She went wild on a cooking spree, much to the delight and enjoyment of everyone in the house. Her aloofness tended to keep people at a distance, as if she didn't want anyone to know her really well. I didn't appreciated Jean's bluntness at first, and I still think she was too critical of others and of situations. However, I began appreciating her more each day.

Arwilda Bryant was the youngest of us all. She was 22 and another beautiful Black girl. She was from Miniola, Texas and had a brother also in the Peace Corps here in Ethiopia. He was teaching in Addis. Arwilda taught typing, shorthand, and bookkeeping. We went into hysteria periodically about her teaching typing on pictures of keyboards! Typewriters were to arrive eventually. Arwilda was very sweet and kind to everyone. She also was not too interested in housework, but she was constantly decorating her room to make it very feminine. I wanted her to show me how to make her lovely smocked pillows.

Marian Lynch, another Black girl, was the last roommate, besides me, of course. She was to teach homemaking classes. However, she had some blood condition that was aggravated by the altitude, so we were told, and had to leave in November. She was given a job at the Peace Corps office in D.C. After she left, Jean and I drew straws for Marian's room. I won. Now each of us remaining had a room of her own!.

Neither Arwilda nor Carolyn drink nor smoke, so I feel most comfortable with them. We were asked if we wished to change our living quarters and we voted to remain together until the next school year.

My assignment was eighth grade English, I had taught English in Milwaukee, but not as an ESL class. In Ethiopia, the eighth grade exam must be passed in order to go on to the secondary school. The previous year only one person had passed. I prayed that many of my students would be successful in mastering English skills.

Our house had been painted and cleaned just for us. There was no real kitchen since Ethiopians do most of their cooking outdoors. We didn't have any sink, stove, or icebox. Fortunately, most of us had bought hot-plates in Addis and our electricity had been working well. We boiled our water and cooked meals on our hot-plates. I made the first meal—a beef roast with gravy, boiled potatoes, and cabbage. Dessert was fudge. Tasty! Every window in our house opened to a spectacular view of the breath-taking mountains.

Four of the fellows had a lovely house about a kilometer from us, and the other five guys were housed three kilometers away. They had a jeep for getting to school and for transporting us once in awhile. Our home was about a kilometer from school over a very rocky dirt road. We'd certainly get our exercise! The two married couples' homes were near the school. A third couple had experienced culture shock and had already returned to the U.S. Now we were 18 PCV's in Dessie.

We had planned to do all of our own shopping, cooking, cleaning, and laundry ourselves, just as we would in the U.S. However, when we visited the market place to buy groceries (onions, potatoes, cabbage, eggs, bananas, oranges, and other staples), we discovered that each purchase took forever since we had to haggle over every price. Suddenly, children came running from everywhere. They called out, "Ferengi!" (foreigner) while stepping all over venders' blankets and ruining produce. Being the cause of a near riot made us rethink our original plan. We decided that we'd be helping the Ethiopian economy if we hired a cook and housekeeper. We already had a "zebunya' or guard, who came with the house. Our zebunya, Mogus, was a little old man who worked twenty-four hours a day. No one seemed to know where he lived or slept, but it was our guess that he lived in the blanket he always wore wrapped around him. His job was to keep wandering animals out of our yard, keep people from breaking in while we were gone, and to protect our wood pile. Mogus' Amharic was difficult to understand, but he was good at pantomiming.

Going to the meat market, or butchery, was easier, but more distasteful. Our butchery was a little "store" that looked somewhat like a tool room of a garage only much smaller and not as clean. Inside, and viewable from the road, were sides of various aanimals, hanging all around. Only a dim light from outside came through the door and one small glassless window. One had to look closely at the meat, which was slaughtered about every three days to keep it fresh. Fortunately, the climate here was rather cool, so that the meat didn't spoil too rapidly. After looking at the sides and legs of animal carcasses, we pointed to a piece that looked fairly good, and haggled over the price. The proprietor than took out a vicious-looking saber with remains of other cuttings on it, and skillfully sliced off the piece of our choosing. He neatly wrapped it in newspaper. We carried our purchase home amidst a swarm of flies. Our particular butchery had his meat screened in, which is quite unusual for our village. Most meat markets swarm with flies, inside and out. We habitually scrubbed our meat carefully before thoroughly cooking it.

The children in town always wanted to carry our packages home for us just so they could learn a few English words. In turn, they taught us some Amharic as they accompanied us. Everyone was friendly and we were greeted in Amharic by all we passed on the roads.

The panoply of sights and sounds, when walking any road, was fascinating—a flock of sheep, goats, oxen, cows, or a person leading a donkey train; a young boy with a bleating lamb or goat across his shoulders; men carrying a dozen or more chickens with their legs tied together hanging upside-down and squawking loudly; people stopping to shake hands and gently bowing to each other; women shading themselves with colorful umbrellas. I frequently felt as if I had stepped into a page of *National Geographic*. I ceaselessly wondered how these beautiful, gentle people had existed in this state without advancing for the past three thousand years. There were many beggars, leppers, young and old alike. At first, I wanted to turn my head away. However, their eyes danced delightfully when I smiled and gave the Amharic greeting, "Tena Yestalin" (May God give you health.) Being acknowledged seemed to mean as much to these poor people as money in the palm.

Several Sudan Interior Mission (S.I.M.) people came to fetch me on my first Sunday in Dessie. Their leprosarium was about eight kilometers from Dessie. I spent the day with them, touring the leprosarium, and having a Western lunch and dinner. The fellowship was wonderful. They brought fresh vegetables to town for all the PCV's and invited the whole group to visit the leprosarium at Boro Meda for a picnic. They opened their homes and their hearts readily and regularly to the whole PCV group in Dessie. In turn, our Peace Corps group saw the missionaries' simple, sincere love for the leppers, and many of our group made regular visits to Boro Meda. When time came for our group to choose a summer project, almost a dozen of the

PCV's asked to help build a school for the leppers.

Perhaps it was just the wonderful taste of home-cooked meals that brought members of our Dessie crowd again and again to the leprosarium. Perhaps it was the friendliness of the missionaries there. Perhaps it was a place of familiar refuge in a foreign land for others. Whatever it was our Peace Corps contingent had opportunities to see God's love at work in a more tangible manner than most would have experienced back home.

CHAPTER 8
SCHOOL BEGINS

The first day of school at Woizero Siheen was unlike the first day of school anywhere I have been. The school compound was crowded with students and teachers, no one knowing exactly what was to happen next. None of us had received class programs, no student lists, and no room assignments. Even the Headmaster looked confused to me. We were finally given a blank sheet of paper on which to register our students, and a room number. When we reported to our rooms, no students were there.

My room was in a brick building with the usual tin roof. The small room had double seated wooden benches with desks attached. There was a small chalkboard behind the table and chair for the teacher. Across the room opposite the entrance, were a series of glass windows, with L-shaped cranks for opening them. They overlooked a beautiful green, cavernous valley. The interior was, otherwise, bare—no book cases, no books, no waste basket—bare. Later, I was to learn that there was no need for a waste basket. There was no "waste" paper. Every scrap of paper was picked up and put to use—sometimes for wall decorations, sometimes folded into a cone shape and used in the place of a bag. It was taken to the market place for salt or sugar to be measured into the conical container. We had a lot to learn about conservation from these practical people.

We all waited in empty rooms for sometime. Finally we returned to the Headmaster's office. Here students milled around, waiting to be registered. One of the older, regular members of the faculty told us that many of the students would take four or more days to arrive since they were coming on foot or by horseback from distant villages over the mountains. We were then dismissed to return the following Monday. This was the easiest first day of school I'd ever had! Much like the Spanish word "manana," Ethiopians have a saying, "isshe nega" which means, "perhaps tomorrow." Everything, even school, seemed to be "isshe nega" around here. There always seemed to be plenty of time to get things done: or to get nothing done!

With several free days, my roommate, Jean Boetcher, and I bought little wooden tables for the bedroom we shared. They had to be sanded, so I put on my jeans and sat out in the yard with some sand paper and proceeded to sand away. Everyone passing stopped to stare, which had become a common occurrence. People seemed to think that my sanding a table was quite an astounding feat for a woman. Before long there were five little boys eager to help me. Since I was becoming bored with my task, I willingly let them help. They vigorously sanded while simultaneously giving me a lesson in Amharic. I taught them some English words.

Then Jean and I decided to take a gherry ride to the Dessie Jail where the prisoners wove and sold beautiful baskets for their own up-keep. Riding a gherry is quite an experience. The gherry is a very small horse drawn cart. The seat is not much bigger than a yardstick in all dimensions. It is perched on spider web-like, bicycle wheels with no place to hang on. The skeletal horse, that pulled the gherry, did not look as if it had eaten in years. While riding on the gherry, I felt like a combination of a chariot rider in ancient Rome, and a Santa Claus on display in a Christmas parade. People stared and waved at us! I'll be glad when people get used to us being here. I've never felt so much like I had three heads, six arms and legs, a dozen tails and plaid skin. Most foreign visitors to this area are men, so we females really get stared at.

When we arrived home after our afternoon's expedition, we found a sink being installed in the kitchen. The water still wasn't hooked up, but this looked promising. We had been buying donkey loads of water: four five gallon nug oil cans full of water from a nearby river. This water had to be boiled and filtered to be safe for drinking, cooking, and brushing teeth. Each household was provided with a water filter—a large metal container with a filtering system inside, looking somewhat like a party-size coffee pot for twenty.

In the evening, most of us girls sat in front of our little fireplace warming ourselves with a cheery blaze. The woven chairs we had purchased were drawn close to the fire to ward off the chilly night air. Jean had popped corn and had her radio turned on to the BBC. We wrote letters under the dim lighting, which went out all together from a thunder storm. I had bought a kerosene lamp just yesterday. It sure came in handy. All of us had indoor plumbing and electricity. In fact, the bathroom in our house had what looked like two commodes! We all thought the one with the faucet was for washing feet. It wasn't until sometime later that a visitor explained what a bidet was for. Naiveté is wonderful!

Because of a night of rain, it was impossible to get to church on Sunday. I sat at the window of my room looking at the beautiful green hills, which were beginning to turn yellow from the lovely little meskal flower, for which Ethiopia is noted. Beneath my window several hens pecked at the grass. I could hear a cow lowing contentedly while grazing on the front lawn. From time to time one of the sheep, out of a flock, which had jumped across the low stone wall into our yard, peered around the corner of the house. A few yards down the road I could see an Ethiopian woman in her snowy white shamma laying clothing on the grass to dry. It amazed me to see how white their clothing stayed! Behind her house, in a chica (mud) kitchen with no door, I could see a servant, wearing a type of gunny sack dress, squatting over a fire on the ground and pouring a mixture for injerra onto a large, round griddle. Little dark-skinned children wearing loose-fitting, dingy white dresses, were running around the yard playing with a dog. In the distance, I could hear Ethiopian boys counting

47

"...and...hulet...sost..." (1,2,3) and laughing, apparently playing some game. Beyond this tranquil busy-ness, stretching as far as the eye could see, were the ever magnificent, rolling green hills with changing shadows cast from fluffy white clouds scuttling across the heavens. The vistas reminded me of Ernest Hemingway's *Green Hills of Africa*.

That evening, some of us discussed our concerns about the seeming lack of progress in this ancient empire. People still built and lived in the same type of grass huts they had lived in for thousands of years. Other rectangular home often sagged because no cross beams were used in construction. There was some electricity and some electrical outlets in our homes, a few in the rectangular houses, but none in the grass huts. Low wattage bulbs could be seen at night in some of the shops in town. Water was obtained from local rivers. Most of it was carried by women in clay water jugs, strapped to their backs or foreheads and weighing close to forty pounds. The lives of women were very difficult. Most were married before puberty. They were bearing babies while still being children themselves. This contributed to making these women age prematurely. Almost everything was carried on backs or shoulders, no matter how heavy. Few had heard of a simple wheelbarrow, which could make many jobs easier. I sometimes found it difficult to even watch because I could almost feel the weight of the object being carried.

Women seldom laughed. Children and men laughed, but very seldom the women. Even then it was often, a quiet, suppressed laughter. The life of the majority of the women in this country appeared to be very difficult: betrothed before puberty; bearing six to eight children, of which two or three survive; transporting heavy loads on their backs daily; marketing; cooking; laundry; animal and child care. Everything had to be done under the harshest of conditions. No wonder women looked ancient by thirty years of age.

Then there was the prevailing attitude of "isshe nega"—there is no hurrying for any reason whatsoever: what gets done, gets done; what doesn't, doesn't; tomorrow is fine. There appeared to be no concept of time nor maintenance. "Isshe nega" could be a contributing factor to keeping a three thousand year old country still living in mud homes as they did thousands of years ago.

As a whole the Ethiopians appeared to be a polite, quiet, reserved people, only coming to life when discussing their children or haggling over a price. I could see why many African students, who were educated in America, were reluctant to return to their villages. There is little to return to. Family units seem to be more filled with respect for each other, out of the need for survival, than love. Once a young person enters high school and obtains four years of college, he has lost contact with most relatives. Letters sent to homes or villages in remote areas are often kept unopened for lengthy periods, waiting for someone to come who can read, and even longer for someone who can write a letter in response. Being spoiled by Western culture, only the most altruistic of the educated usually wish to return to their roots, where they possibly could make a difference.

Finally, on Monday, more students had arrived at our school. Many more were still expected. I began teaching English with my classes of 22 to 26 students, each. I spent the first two days talking to my classes so that they could get use to my accent. They were very responsive and appeared to be understanding my English.

The school day began with meeting in our homerooms for attendance. We proceeded to the field for the raising of the Ethiopian flag, singing their national anthem, and prayers led by a Christian student and a Muslim student. All were then dismissed single file to class. Instead of students passing from class to class, the teachers did the passing from room to room throughout the day. The students stayed in the same room all day long.

When a teacher entered the room, the entire class stood and remained standing until the teacher was seated. Since many American teachers tend to walk around or stay standing, we had to regularly remind our students to be seated. We carried our own chalk and a sock for an eraser with us since no equipment was in any room. Every time a student was called upon, he stood. I only had two to six girls in any of my classes since most girls are married by age thirteen and taking care of a husband and children. The ages of students ranged from twelve to thirty in any one class. Many of the young men could not begin school at a younger age, since they were needed to help tend the flocks or farm the land. Bare feet are more common than shoes. I was always afraid I'd step on toes. The students appeared to be neat in appearance, as neat as can be expected under the living conditions in Ethiopia.

By the second week of the first semester, students had arrived and my classes were 36-40 students each. The students used composition books for their assignments and were eager to try all work. Much oral work, vocabulary building, and sentence combinations were attacked by all with great enthusiasm. All were so eager to please. I had to slow down my speech patterns to accommodate my learners. There were enough language barriers to put obstacles in the way of teaching and learning. Yet, the child-like eagerness to feast on everything I said, was humbling. I soon learned that students had Amharic names for me: Woizerite Baga (Miss Summers, my maiden name), Icafash (you are laughter), and Tsahainesh (you are sunshine). All three names were used periodically, but Tsahainesh was the name most students and villagers called me throughout my stay in Ethiopia.

Our faculty at Woizero Siheen consisted of fifteen Indian teachers (one a woman), twenty-three Ethiopian teachers (two women), and our *nineteen PCV's (eight women). We were friendly, but everyone seemed to be a little shy of each other. I prayed that we would mix well instead of staying in our own comfortable little groups. My household of girls hoped to soon have an open house for our faculty.

*19 PCV's changed to 18 after Marian Lynch left in November.

CHAPTER 9
STUDENTS: CONTRASTING VISITS

Three students were crammed into each double bench with approximately one square foot of space for each pupil's use. There was one dim light bulb hanging from the ceiling in our dark stone room, but on sunny days it was quite bright with sunlight pouring in through the windows. As I looked at my students, with their variety of patched clothing, various odors, and bare feet, I sensed their eagerness to learn and felt their apprehension about passing the eighth grade examination, upon which hinges so much of their future. I was told that only one student had passed the previous year. I was also told not to expect much participation in the classroom from my charges.

What amazement and joy I experienced when my classes all voluntarily took part in discussions, answering questions, and writing on the board. In fact, their spontaneity took me by surprise. I had never seen so many hands come up at one time in response to my questions. Information that I disseminated in morning classes, was often reviewed, shared, and memorized by more than half of the class by the afternoon sessions. Even the five or six girls in every one of my classes were taking part in discussions. I had heard that the girls were almost invisible in our classrooms. Perhaps they felt bolder with a woman teacher.

The students also liked to tease and be teased. One day in a class of six girls and thirty young men, I discovered that somehow, that day, I had seven girls and twenty-nine fellows. The girls' heads, as usual, were covered with shawls, under which dark eyes peeked out. Often, a portion of the shawl was even held over the mouth. This was true today of the seven girls, while the guys, with eyes dancing, waited to see my response. When I laughingly indicated that one of the "girls" looked a bit masculine under the swaddling shawl, the class burst into laughter.

Another time an annoying fly kept buzzing past my mouth. Flies were everywhere and many students carried "fly whisks," "horse tail whisks," or a short, leafy branch to fan away flies from their faces. During a discussion, I happened to take a deep breath and swallowed a big, black fly. My facial expression must have indicated to the class that the fly had passed over my tongue, and, with my hands at my throat, I felt the last of its buzzing before fully swallowing it. The bursts of laughter were more compassionate this time, as students all commiserated their own insect ingestions.

Ato Yifru Gebayu, our headmaster, reminded me that a girls' club might be beneficial to our female enrollment. Girls, I had been told, never participated in any school activity. Few remained in school after the eighth grade, since they were betrothed and married by fifteen, often much younger. Before my ideas for the club could gel, they were waylaid by an unusual occurrence at school.

The most outstanding student in all my classes was a beautiful teenager by the name of Lakech Ali. She was not intimidated by any of the boys. Everyone seemed to respect her as a person, admired her intelligence, and appreciated her eagerness to help everyone. Her beauty and sweetness were enhanced by the knowledge that she came from one of the poorer homes. All of Dessie seemed to want to see this young girl succeed.

During one of the afternoon classes, I saw Lakech's head down on her arms. Since Lakech had always been an active participant in class, I asked the girl sitting next to her if Lakech was ill. I thought I heard the girl say that Lakech had a "headache." I asked if she wished to go to our school clinic, but she declined. When the bell rang for the end of the day, Lakech tried to stand up but was so unsteady that she had to sit back down. I went over to her where a group of girls were all looking concerned. This time she explained that her heart was racing, causing pain and difficulty breathing. With several students assisting, we started carrying her to the clinic. She passed out in our arms on the way, and we had to carry her.

Her attack was diagnosed as heart failure. I was told that this had happened at least ten times before. During summer, she had gone to Addis for a cardiogram. The doctor had told her not to work too hard; to eat more fruit, vegetables, and drink milk—expensive fare for most Ethiopians. Lakech lived with two married sisters, and she earned ten dollars a month tutoring. This was her sole support. Injerra and wat, her usual food, was not the most nourishing for her.

The next day, after school, some of the girls took me to visit our ill friend. We loaded up with fresh fruits and vegetables and some books. Her home was a grass hut some distance from school. As we left the main road, we climbed over rocks in a section of town where the grass shacks were very close together. We had to walk single file to pass between them. Many of these homes were so small that most of the families sat outside, making our passage even narrower. After nearly stepping on a dozen chickens and several children, and almost being run over by a cow coming down our path, we finally stopped in front of a hut.

Here was where Lakech lived. There was no door. We clambered over several rocks and bent over to go through an opening. The sarbet (grass house) was made out of sticks held together with dung. There was no window. The only light was from the cooking fire on the floor and the open doorway. The interior was no bigger than a small bedroom, and the whole family lived here! A rustic bench occupied one side of the room. One of the students motioned to a pallet on the floor in the darkest part of the room. Here was Lakech. I went over and handed her the produce and the books, which she shyly accepted. I told her and her sisters that food like this was needed. I appointed several girls to help me get these thing for her on a regular basis. A sister in a dirty gunny sack dress, smiled with embarrassment and pleasure at my visit to this poor area of town. I noticed a crowd gathering at the doorway. Warm milk was offered to me, which I declined, stating Lakech was more in need of it. I did politely accept the hot steaming tea.

While visiting, I told the girls the story of Cinderella, using a few Ethiopian adaptations—an angel instead of a fairy Godmother, a lovely gherry in the place of a golden carriage, hyenas instead of mice, and Jubilee Palace for the home of the handsome Ras or prince. The girls with me translated the tale to all at the door, who "aahh'ed" and clapped. The tale was vastly enjoyed by all. It was time to leave.

My visit was quite an event for the neighborhood. Crowds of women in the same type of dirty, gunny-sack dress, scantily clad children, and a number of men had stuck their heads in the doorway. They thronged the narrow pathway, calling out "Tsahainesh" as I passed. Part of me felt like a circus side-show, and part of me ached for the poverty that encircled me. What had been my own impoverished background, now appeared to me to be wealthy beyond the wildest dreams of these sweet, gentle peasants. How accepting they were of God's plan for them. The Amharic word for "God" was generously used in most conversations. In thankfulness, I praised God for my simple family, home and education.

On our way home, one of the other girls begged me to stop at her house and meet her mother. This house was much larger with a wooden door, glass windows, and several rooms. Her father was the director at Asfaw Wossen Hospital in Dessie, which explained their affluence. Her mother and I conversed in Amharic. I was served tea and dabbo, a type of bread.

What a contrast these two visits had been!

CHAPTER 10
DISTURBING HOME-FRONT NEWS

October of 1962 brought distressing news from America regarding the Civil Rights Movement. Students and faculty heard of the difficulties Blacks in the U. S. were having with voter registration. It had come to a crisis in Mississippi with the deaths of three young men, who had been helping to register Blacks to vote in elections. Everyone interrogated us on the issues. How could this happen in a democracy? Our hearts were full of remorse on the problems facing us back home. There was no justification for the actions of those who found it so difficult to accept change. Too many actions were abhorrent to us. I did not want to be associated with narrow-minded white bigots. We took courage in speeches of Martin Luther King, Jr. and his non-violent movement. Ethiopia greatly respected John F. Kennedy, and they admired his out-spoken brother, Robert, too. Many here were aware that both political figures stood strongly for Civil Rights.

Here, teaching in the midst of an Empire, ruled by a despot, benevolent or not, it was easy to see the enormity of the problems facing this country, which was trying to emerge onto the world scene. We heard voices of dissent from students and adults wishing to have a greater voice in the direction of their country. Some condemned their Emperor for not sharing power as he had previously promised his nation. The most vociferous were exiled to towns far from the capital.

How arrogant of Americans to condemn others, especially those less fortunate than themselves! The speck of a problem we see in struggling areas of the world, seldom compares with the Redwood log, sticking out of the eye of a number of people in our own country.

CHAPTER 11
THE DESSIE GROUP

There were absolutely no nicer PCV's than the group here in Dessie. In addition to my five housemates, about whom I have written, there were two households of fellows. In the closest house, about a kilometer away, were four guys: Gene Rosachi and Jerry Lemmert from Oregon and they were both about 30. Gene appeared to be the only Catholic in our group and he attended a church here regularly with the Italian family who was in charge of the Dessie Hotel. He was rather quiet but an excellent cook. He invited us over regularly to enjoy his kiitchen creations. He also brought with him the record, "Camelot," which I had almost worn out. Gene was teaching English. Jerry was a science teacher. He gathered every kind of insect, flower and leaf for a collection. He also had an aviary of 20 different wild birds. Jerry tended to be quiet. We discovered him to also be a good mechanic. One of the Peace Corps jeeps rested at their compound. Marc Clausen was from Arizona and taught agriculture at our school. He had practically set up a whole farm with horses, chickens, turkeys, and rabbits. Marc was from a Methodist background. George Parish, from North Carolina, was the comic in the group. It took a while for us to get used to his sense of humor. Some thought he was a hypochondriac, but that was because he was in charge of all the Peace Corps medicine for our group. George taught history and math. That comprised that interesting household.

In the house some distance away from the school resided five more fellows. Don Kilhefner, about 25, was from Pennsylvania and had his

Master's Degree. He was teaching history. His humor was quite contagious. He called himself a skeptic on religion, feeling there was nothing about which one could be certain. David Hurst, also about 25, was from a small town in Kansas. He was tall, had very red hair and was very realistic about life. He was teaching shop classes, and was an outstanding mechanic. The second of our jeeps was housed with this group. John Bigelow, also around the same age as the other two, was from Washington, and said that his father was a lawyer, his mother, a folk singer. He played most instruments and liked to sing. He appeared to be the intellectual of our group, and said everything must be reasoned out, when we talked about religion. Faith appeared to be incomprehensible to him. However, he asked me if I had an extra *Bible* with me.which I passed on to him. He was a science-math teacher. Otto Rink was a little bitty guy from Texas. I don't think he weighed more than 90 pounds, but he had great sense of humor. I guess not everything from Texas was big! He also had very blond hair which had become bleached white by the African sun. The students wanted to know if he was the oldest one in the Peace Corps. He was only 25. Otto's family was from Germany and they were all musicians. Otto was teaching instrumental music. Ron Bell had his M.A. in music. He and Otto lived, ate and breathed music. Ron was from Michigan and had toured around the world with the University of Michigan's band. Ron was a real wholesome person and friendly with everyone. Ron and Otto discovered a building full of instruments on the school compound. They taught a number of students how to play them, and a marching band was formed. Ron also was elected to be our spokesman for the PCV's in Dessie.

There were also two couples: the Mirkins and the Embreys. Each had their own homes a bit closer to the school. Lois Mirkin wore no make-up and had long dark hair. She tried to teach Cora and me how to knit. I was not very good at it. Harris Mirkin was prematurely grey. The couple was from New York City and reminded us all of beatniks. They had all kinds of modern art on their walls, interesting bottle arrangements, and folk music playing all the time. Lois and Harris called themselves chefs and enjoyed acquainting themselves with all the Ethiopian spices. The Mirkins played guitar which, both had brought with them. Many evenings and most of our parties included the singing of folk songs: "Blowing in the Wind," "If I Had a Hammer," "Five Hundred Miles," "House of the Rising Sun," and so many more. The Mirkins had an enormous repitoire. The Embreys were also very artistic. They were a very attractive couple and easy going.

Our Ethiopia I Peace Corps group came with many skills beside teaching. We all got along well and enjoyed working together for our first year.

Almost every household took in several students. We all discovered young people who had no home in Dessie. Some were as much as a six day walk from the nearest relative. One example was Belay Gabre, who came from a village high above Dessie, at an elevation of 16,000 feet. Like so many others, he had never worn shoes, seen electric lights, nor seen a motorized vehicle

Education was so desired that young boys were willing to curl up in a blanket at night, huddle close to a wall, and sleep in the chilly mountain air. Odd jobs or begging for food from kind villagers would keep them going. We established a hot lunch program at school. But some kids still needed a place to sleep. Most of us had structures behind our houses where we built bunk beds and took in five or six young men. We fed, clothed, and housed them. They, in turn, chopped wood, ran errands, helped with translations, and did innumerable jobs for us.

One of the most treasured items our boys received from their benefactors was a pair of shoes. All had gone barefoot prior to this gift. It was a pleasure to see their delight on the presentation of this piece of clothing to them. We had already given them several changes of trousers, shorts, and shirts. We saw them wear all the items of clothing regularly—except the shoes. Some of our Ethiopian and Indian co-workers had called our purchases "foolish.' They told us the students would turn around and sell things we gave them, especially shoes. Since we hadn't seen the boys wearing anything on their feet, we became a bit suspicious. We finally called the young men together and asked if they were disappointed in the shoes we had given them. "Oh, no," they all stated as they ran to get their most prized possession. They returned to us with the shoes tied together and slung over their shoulders. "We love them and are proud to have them, but we only wear them on very special occasions. You see, if we wear them a lot, the soles of our feet, which are very tough from walking barefoot since birth, will grow tender. Then we will need shoes all the time. When you leave, we may never get shoes again. These are very special to us."

How easy it is to make a judgment when one only knows part of a story.

In addition to taking in students, our Dessie PCV group enjoyed many jaunts around the countryside in our two jeeps. The day after the big faculty party, we got up at six in the morning for a trek to the Danikil Desert. We took the beautiful mountain road down from Dessie to Cambolsha, which is about twenty kilometers down a very steep road filled with hair-pin turns. From Cambolsha, we turned off to a small town named Boti, which had a large sprawled out market place. The market took place one day a week. From Boti we dropped down to the floor of the desert. The temperature rose thirty to forty degrees. The Danikil tribe inhabited this arid place. They were a nomadic people, who carried all their belongings on their camels, and the women wore nothing above the waist, although a turban often shaded their heads. One of the guys stated, "Maiden-form bra company would go wild here!" The Danikil women, in turn, stared at the girls in our group, pointing their fingers at our blouses, and cackled. There was no way *we* were going native!

An Ethiopian teacher, who accompanied us, said that the Danikil did not eat meat. They lived on the camel's milk and the butter they made from it. If an animal died, they just skinned it, and left the bones

59

and carcass behind. They drained the blood and let it congeal. Mixed with milk it became another part of their diet. A skinned carcass was on the side of the road as we came down the mountain. On our way back up, we saw the remains, picked clean by vultures. Only the bleached white skeleton of a cow, with its ribcage poking up to the sky, graced the side of the road.

We continued our drive beyond the area of the Danikil, beyond the bushy, scrubby part of the desert. We drove out to level sandy, flat areas where gazelle, ostriches, and long-horned cattle roamed freely. I sat on the hood of one of the jeeps as we chased animals, feeling as if I were in the movie, *Hatari*. On the way back, we stopped at a little thatched house. It had a generator-run refrigerator with COLD Coca Cola—a true oasis in the desert! However, I had to relieve myself and there were no johns. Another girl went with me to find a secluded place. We finally found a bush and took turns watching for each other. As I was relieving myself, I felt something staring at me. I looked up into the faces of a herd of goats. They stared at me with great curiosity!

On our way back, we stopped at a small Danikil market where dozens of tribal warriors squatted under the shade of acacia trees. They wore brightly colored wraps tied around the waist, and swords strapped to their sides. Tall spears were held upright in their hands. They looked rather ferocious. We decided to bargain with them for some spears. As we stood in the shade and looked out at the heat waves dancing on this vast desert plain; as we looked at the strange desert tribesmen surrounding us on all sides, we had a sense of the exotic adventure we were all experiencing.

Many times during our stay in Dessie, we returned to this and other colorful market places. We attended many holiday celebrations, weddings, and parties together. We became well acquainted during the twelve hour jeep rides to Addis for picking up supplies. Some of us hitch-hiked on a Swedish cargo liner from the ports of Massawa to Asab on the Red Sea. Others flew to Alexandria, Egypt and traveled down the Nile River to Cairo, Luxor, Thebes, Abu Simbul, and Khartoom. During our second Christmas in the country, a group of us went to Jerusalem and Damascus. We traveled cheap, staying in pensions, and sometimes sleeping on our towels along the banks of the Nile River or on the banks of the Red Sea, using our duffel bags for pillows. Enjoying each other's company, we were always ready to tackle another adventure and to develop special lifetime attachments.

CHAPTER 12
OTHER PCV WEEKEND ACTIVITIES

Some weekends, groups of PCV's drove to Addis Abeba for supplies. Some weekends were spent correcting papers, making lesson plans, and entertaining the multitude of people who dropped in on us. Other weekends were filled with hikes and explorations of our surroundings. Still others were occupied with visiting the nearby Lutheran Mission or the Sudan Interior Mission with its leprosarium. We also planned special holiday celebrations for ourselves.

Six of us piled into a jeep after school on a Friday for our periodic trip to get supplies for everyone, fill up on necessary medicines like our weekly dosage of Aralen to ward off malaria, several antibiotics, and various cleaning materials not available in our village. The first trip I went on didn't leave Dessie until midnight. Our Jeep ran out of gas about four in the morning. Since it was still dark out, and we had seen five hyenas along the road, we could not send anyone ahead to a station for gas, especially since the nearest station was at least ten kilometers away. We had to sit for three hours before a truck came along and could take one of the fellows to a station for gas. We were finally refueled by eight-thirty in the morning and arrived in Addis by ten-thirty. We spent the complete day getting our supplies and loading our Jeep to capacity. Needless-to-say, we purchased gerry cans to fill with gasoline, so future trips might avoid our kind of delay. The Peace Corps made accommodations for us at a good hotel and we slept a few hours before we were on our way back to Dessie at four in the morning on Sunday.

We decided to explore the Danikil Desert again for a short side-trip. A huge market had been set up. There, in the middle of the market place was a gallows with two male bodies hanging. Violent criminals were made an example for all to heed. To distract myself, I thought I would try bargaining for a camel. Off to the side of the market place was the "parking lot" for camels, donkeys, and horses. As I walked around one of the camels, with its legs tucked under him in a sitting position, calmly chewing its cud with huge swings of its lower jaw, I was asked if I wanted to purchase the animal. When I asked how much the camel cost, the man in a long caftan, which looked much like a cotton striped nightshirt, said one hundred dollars. I stated that I wouldn't want to pay more than ten dollars for the animal. The man stared at me unblinkingly, then stated, "He is worth at least $75.00"

I walked around the camel and pointed out that its hair was coming out in huge clumps and I wouldn't consider more than $12.00 for it.

"You wish to take the food out of the mouths of my wife and children!" the owner whined with his arms outstretched supplicatingly. Then calmly he said "Perhaps I might consider $60.00."

I almost felt guilty as I walked up to the camel's head pretending I knew a lot about this type of animal. It just continued to monotonously chew. "The teeth look very old," I said. "I wouldn't pay more that $15.00 for an old camel."

"You are a thief!" the seller shouted, just as a commotion was detected beyond the "parking lot."

Apparently, a camel owner near this area, had been prodding his reclining camel with a sharp stick, attempting to get the beast up. As he began to whip the animal, the camel moaned deeply in his throat, slowly thrust up his front legs and then the rear ones. It stood pawing the sand with the enormous pads on the bottom of its paws, raising dust and bellowing through its nostrils and mouth. His owner seemed to know that he had gone too far, and began backing away from the front of the camel. With a mighty shake of its head, the creature eyed the object of its torture.

Turning to run, the owner began to race across the empty desert, looking back at the camel he had just abused. With long legged strides, the camel began to lope after its tormentor. The hundreds in the market place watched the drama unfold with growing grins on their faces. A rock loomed ahead of the camel abuser, and he proceeded to strip himself of his caftan, leaving it in the open while he hid his naked body behind the outcropping. The snorting, bawling camel halted in its stride at the garment on the ground. Placing an enormous padded foot on the cloth, the camel began to shred the material with its teeth, trumpeting out with each tear as it shook the garment with its head, leaving nothing but threads on the ground. When the animal's anger had subsided, it pawed the shreds once more, turned back towards the market place, shook its head and body, then proudly ambled back to the spot where it had been resting before the rude interruption.

From behind the rock, the owner, modestly bent over, crept to the pile of rags. He lifted the remains of his garment and tied what he could around his waste. As he made his way apologetically back to his camel, laughter and shouts rang out from various areas of the market. We were told that people were calling to the owner to be nicer to his "friend." Apparently, several had noticed him tormenting his camel lately. Animals and people need to be treated kindly. It was time for us to finish our drive home. My bargaining was forgotten as we climbed into the Jeep.

Our complete ride was once again spectacular. The beauty of the mountains, valleys rivers, waterfalls, and the simplicity of the people along the way was constantly new to all of us. Women carrying umbrellas to shade them from the intense sun, Galla women with water jugs strapped to their backs, men with loads that should be carried by three people, all flanked either side of the roadway. In other places, hyenas, gazelles, rabbits, owls, ducks could be seen from the road. From Addis to Dessie, our Jeep traveled through a branch of the Great Rift Valley. We went down one mountain and up another, numerous times. Then for a long time we stayed on the floor of the Rift

Valley, circling around the base of several mountains. Finally, the car neared a steep ascent and the road made dozens of hair-pin turns as we climbed up to Dessie. Drop-offs of 3000 feet followed along the side of our narrow, unmaintained road. The views of neighboring mountains towering over us and then dropping off again into verdant valleys, left us breathless. Occasionally we saw children perched on the edge of thousand foot drop-offs. This made some of us a bit nervous. As we came over the rise that descended into Dessie, there were donkey caravans, herds of cattle and goats blocking our way. We waited until the herd driver chased them to the side so we could continue.

All of our trips to Addis were eventful. One time a thirty foot snake lay alongside the road. A group of men, one with a "Father New Year" type scythe, danced around the snake. We stopped our Jeep and the men explained how the snake had been stealing baby lambs and goats over a period of time. They had staked a baby lamb on a rope in the middle of a grassy field and waited for the thief to slither through the tall grass. Once the lamb had passed through the jaws of the serpent, the snake was temporarily immobilized. The men then jumped out and hacked just behind the head of the snake. They were able to kill their culprit and save the young victim.

With the rainy season over, it was torture to stay indoors. The beautiful weather made us all adventurous and eager to be off investigating the beauty that surrounded us. However, we were here as teachers. This meant lesson plans and lots of papers to correct. Thus, we had to discipline ourselves. In the midst of our required tasks, we were regularly interrupted by visitors. The Headmaster of Negus Michael School, an elementary school in Dessie, stopped to introduce us to an elderly man, whom he thought would make a good servant for us. The man, Kebede, had worked for Europeans and knew our style of cooking. He was good at marketing and had excellent references. We made an appointment at the local hospital for him to get an examination. We ended up hiring him for forty dollars a month. Incredible!

A little later that same day two of the Peace Corps fellows dropped in for an hour. Soon after they left, two of the Ethiopian teachers at our school came by for an hour. All the while our guests were here, our phone (number 4 in the village) rang constantly. The Peace Corps fellows called to say that our town would have two Jeeps for us to use. Next they called to say that our air freight luggage had arrived in Addis. Next they called to see if we knew of a plumber in Dessie because their commode had broken in half! We knew the man who had recently installed our kitchen sink, so we were able to help. We seemed to be called constantly for advice on cooking and sewing. You'd think we were authorities. We managed to play the part to the hilt! Since tea was generally served when people dropped in, we had become quite adept as hostesses. This was particularly important since we only had seven cups in the house! One of us had to quickly wash and dry the cups as soon as guests left, and get the pot of water ready for the next round of people. We all became experts at tea diplomacy!

Some weekends one or more of us would be left in Dessie, while the others had the opportunity to visit the capital. Jean and I liked to explore the area we called "our mountain," a view we had from our bedroom window. Two students, Getachew and Saife Zarufael, both with infectious grins, were eager to show us the way to "our mountain." After going up and down several very high hills, we came upon a ravine with a breath-taking sight. A waterfall cascaded with a dull roar over the rocks nearby. A number of people were washing clothes on the banks of the stream. We picked our way down to the bottom of the hill where the stream was fairly swift. Not finding a narrow trail to cross, Getachew found a less rocky spot where the water was only a foot deep. We took off our shoes and socks, rolled up our jeans, and forded the stream. On the other side, we put our socks and shoes back on our wet feet to climb this side of the ravine. When we arrived at what we thought was the top, we saw one rolling hill after another rising up above the rest, with valleys and ravines separating each. Beyond them was "our mountain." We definitely wanted to continue on. On the hillsides grazed sheep, cows, and horses. As we descended, the land became wet and marshy; but as we ascended, the ground became dry and stony. It seemed as if we would never stop ascending and descending. We had more incentive to go on when Saife told us that the side of "our mountain" was covered with monkeys!! Nearing the mountain, we had to pass through a dense stand of eucalyptus trees. We blazed a trail through the woods and came out in a clump of undergrowth, which bordered the foot of the mountain.

As we stood looking up at the rocky cliffs, sure enough, there were hundreds of little and big monkeys scampering all over, dislodging stones in their way and making them fall near our feet with loud cracking noises. As soon as the monkeys spotted us, the chief monkey, a type of baboon with white coloring around his eyes, started barking at us from his high perch on the side of the cliff. Suddenly, hundreds of monkeys from all directions, started heading towards him as if for protection. Dozens of mother monkeys with babies clinging to their backs, went scampering up the side of the mountain. The crevasses and cracks of the cliff became alive with all the activity. Three hundred feet of jumping, leaping mountain towered over us. Oh, to have had a telephoto lens along!

Our walk had been a long arduous one; it was late in the day. Thousands of other mountains tumbled in all directions and beckoned us to come and explore. We reluctantly turned around, promising ourselves to come back and climb "monkey mountain."

The only Protestant church service in Dessie was at the American Lutheran Mission. The Sudan Interior Leprosarium had a service in Amharic, but they were a thirty to forty minute drive out of town. Later, students showed me a direct walking path to the S.I.M., but it was still a two hour hike. The S.I.M. people always drove me home and brought all the PCV's ample supplies of potatoes, corn, and cabbage. However, the Lutheran Mission had their compound behind a walled fortress and it was located right off the Piazza. Their services were usually in English. I learned that some of my male students lived on the compound in a type of youth hostel. The S.I.M. missionaries gave me a dozen Bibles in English and the Lutheran folk said that I could begin a Bible study with the boys living there after the Sunday service. There was an amazing response. Solomon, one of the students living at our house, also joined in with the study. He had been accompanying me to church services regularly.

The Lutheran Mission was very modern. The missionaries' home had a washer and dryer, indoor bath and plumbing, and many conveniences. They also had graciously invited the PCV's to meals. I accepted every invitation that came my way—American or Ethiopian! Most of my household visited the services and stayed for meals periodically. A few of the male PCV's stayed more to themselves. One attended the Catholic Church in town. There was a little pump organ at the Lutheran Church inside the mission. Since I was the only one who admitted to reading a little music, I became the one-finger accompanist at times. During our second year, Ron Bell, the PCV music teacher who had begun a school band, became our choir director. Part of his incentive was the addition of a pretty new female PCV, who enjoyed church services.

The Sudan Interior Mission and Leprosarium really became the "home away from home" for many of the PCV's. The S.I.M. compound was larger and more sprawled out, than the Lutheran Mission. There were no walls surrounding the compound. Two missionary families and two single missionary women lived on the station, each occupying a private home. They frequently chuckled that each house "had four rooms and a path," since they all had a pathway to out-houses around the back. A small washroom was in each home, with a basin, pitcher of water for hygiene, and a chamber pot for night time use. There were also several guest houses, consisting of two bedrooms with a small washroom separating the bedrooms. The guesthouses also had out-houses behind them.

Running the mission station was Dr. Ed Jones, a physician. He and his wife were from Ontario, Canada and were middle aged. Their 14 year old son was in Addis at Bingham Academy, a boarding school for missionary children. Skip and Helen Estelle had four beautiful, well-behavied pre-schoolers. The little children had many young Ethiopian friends and they all chattered together in Amharic. Skip was a graduate of Cornell with a degree in animal husbandry and agriculture. He trained all the Ethiopians on the compound, the leppers being in the majority, in proper growing techniques on their vast farmland. The station was almost self-sufficient, growing enough food for all the leppers, the missionaries, and enough to share great quantities with the PCV's. One of the single women was a delightful British nurse, Beryl Johnson. She took care of the out-patient clinic, where she saw about 200 people daily. She also performed about ten eye, operations a day for trachoma, and delivered babies. Her wonderful accent, sense of humor, and vast repertoire of delicious cookies, kept all of us heading the Jeeps to the Leprosarium. Mavis Fishwick, a widow from Australia with another delightful accent, did most of the leprosy work. She had over 200 patients in the leprosarium and others who constantly came for daily treatment from the countryside. Their work sounded exhausting but they were always so cheerful and friendly.

The following year some of our SIM friends were replaced by other missionaries. I became close to Ruth Shoestrum, who replaced Mavis Fishwick. Other changes also took place, but the PCV's continued to flock out to the leprosarium. They seemed to enjoy these new people almost as much or more than before. I was so thankful that these missionaries, who were kept so busy daily working with the nationals, took time out for all of us from the States. They never treated us as if we were an imposition. Instead, they welcomed us with open arms every time we visited. They even helped us to buy two hogs which they fattened for us. Then they had a dozen of us stay overnight to be able to arise at dawn for the slaughtering, scraping, rendering, cutting, and preparing of the meat. It was a long, tiring day for all. We sure feasted afterwards—hams, porkchops, hamberger, smoked butt, etc. All of us had a little bit of home whenever we were with these people who were so willing to share of themselves and their time.

We learned that most cases of Leprosy (Hanson's disease) could be cured in four years. However, the uneducated villagers often cast the lepper out to become a beggar. The S.I.M. colony took in several hundred afflicted individuals. They helped the leppers to build their own houses on the compound, to construct a large kitchen for feeding everyone, to build looms for weaving, and to instruct everyone in some skill. Some reading was taught to those who had vision and wished to learn. Some writing was taught to those who had hands and wished to learn. Proper hygiene was also included and medicine was dispensed. The aim was to heal and make each individual able to return to his village able to assume a valuable role—farming, animal care, cooking, child care, spinning thread, weaving, becoming the village scribe or reader. Reading and writing were the most difficult to teach since the lepper colony had no school.

Our group became so attached to these wonderful people that we designed our summer project around the Leprosarium—to build a school on the compound. All but three or four of our PCV's joined in on this project. Most had a desire to help the leppers, and wanted to return some greatfulness for everything the missionaries had done for us. Everywhere on the compound we saw gentle care and respect being given by the missionaries to all their patients. In return, one could see respect and affection from the leppers.

On weekends the S.I.M. people invited us to drive out whenever we wished. They always welcomed us with plenty of American food. One weekend when all my housemates had gone to Addis, some of the missionaries had come to town to get their mail. I, along with two of the fellows, George Parish and Marc Clausen, were invited to stay overnight at the Leprosarium. I would stay with the Estelle's and the guys would have one of the guest houses. I was able to use a sewing machine there to make some curtains while the fellows explored the area. Marc was from a Methodist background, but didn't like to talk about religion. George had been active in Youth for Christ, like me, and seemed to hold his church activities in high regard. At the mission compound they would attend Sunday services.

It amazed me how eager my fellow PCV's were to help build a school at the SIM station. So many of the Dessie group were vocal about their disinterest in anything religious and would argue about various Christian tenets. However, their affection for these SIM missionaries was real, and our group knew they had the skills to build the lepper school.

Little did I know at this time that one of these Peace Corps men would become important in my life.

CHAPTER 13
A BRA FOR THE BRALESS—
OUR FACULTY PARTY

We finally hired a cook and a housekeeper. Kebede, our cook, was middle-aged, short and slight in stature. He was married and had a little boy. He had learned to prepare Western food while working for an American family is Addis. We didn't have a refrigerator, but food lasted two to three days because it was cold in October. Kebede did all the shopping and bargaining. His cooking was quite tasty. We had cabbage, carrots, potatoes, onions, or corn with chicken, beef or lamb. Kebede would boil, fry or stew these together or separately to give us variety. He also knew how to bake some breads and cookies. There were freshly baked hard rolls available in some shops in town. We gave him money for his purchases. Marmalade and jam were occasionally for sale in cans in the Arab souks in town. Kebede hovered over us at meals, anticipating our needs and plying us with more food. None of us was used to being waited on at meals. Having someone so solicitous and eager to please us was awkward at times. We, in turn, wanted to please him because it was so nice to have him taking care of the shopping and cooking. Even when things weren't too palatable, we smiled and would request injerra and wat, the traditional Ethiopian foods, for a few days. He would then ask, "American tomorrow?" We had enough variety and were not undernourished. Salads were greatly missed since lettuce and tomatoes were not safe to eat. We all wished to avoid dysentery.

Kebede also ran to open the door when we came home from

school. He answered the door like a butler whenever visitors came to our house.

Debra, a seventeen year old, was hired to do our laundry, ironing, scrubbing, and general housework. We introduced clotheslines to her. Most women carried the laundry down to the river, beat it on the rocks, and let it dry on the ground in the sunlight. We could afford to buy five gallon jerry cans of water, sold by vendors from the backs of their donkeys. These beasts of burden would carry four, five gallon jerry cans at a time, two on each side of the donkey. We became the best customers, buying all four of their five gallon cans at a time. We used it for cooking, bathing, laundry, and cleaning, and all four cans cost only a dollar.

Neither Debra nor Kebede spoke much English, You should see us pantomiming what we wanted them to do. All of us went into hysterics just watching each other! Our two wonderful helpers were very meek, mild and condescending. Their eyes were usually cast down, but they glanced up at us and twinkled at our feeble attempts to speak their language. It was difficult to stand such attentive service. I felt like such a scrounge and very helpless, not being able to do normal chores for myself!

Our house was taking shape. We had bought rugs and made curtains. Inexpensive woven chairs and straw furnishings complemented our few PC issued items. We were ready to party!

The first weekend in November was our faculty party. A great number of the teachers at our school had invited us for dinner or tea. We all wanted to repay them. We bought cases of Fanta (an orange drink) and Coca Cola. All of the PCV's cooked and baked their hearts out. We served hors d'oeuvres of crackers with spreads of cheese, olives and pickles that had come in packages from home. Our main dishes were injerra and wat, a whole roasted lamb, macaroni and cheese, rice, fried chicken, cabbage, string beans, carrots, potato salad, vegetable casserole, and deviled eggs. For desert we had creamed caramel, cakes, donuts, cookies, and fruit. Tea, coffee, Cola,

Fanta, beer and punch were served. The meal was a huge success with the seventy plus in attendance. We borrowed dishes from the Touring Hotel, where we had stayed our first two weeks.

Folding chairs had been borrowed from the school.

After dinner, we sang some folk songs, accompanied by several PVC's who had brought their guitars. The Ethiopians sang some songs in Amharic for us, and one of the Indians sang a Hindi song. We constantly socialized, moving from one group to another, keeping conversations going. This was something never done at the parties we had attended. Most places people just sat or stood leaning and staring uncomfortably around the room. This crowd was talking and visiting with each other in a relaxed atmosphere. Taped music—Harry Belafonte, "Breakfast at Tiffany" and "Hatari" soundtracks—brought by some of our group, was played in the background. The party ended before midnight. Our super Dessie crew shared expenses.

Our help assisted with food and beverages and cleaned up most of the mess. They usually left right after cleaning up following our nightly meals. They seemed to relish this party as much as we did. They were invaluable. A special bonus was given to them to show our gratitude and appreciation for all their help.

One problem existed the day of the party. Kebede had purchased some new clothing; but Debra had only the clothing she wore each day for work. No problem—we gave her a black skirt and a white blouse to wear. Debra, like most Ethiopian women, did not wear a bra. In fact, she had no idea what those strange garments, she had been washing for us, were! We did not think the blouse would look very decent without a bra. So, in the process of measuring her and deciding which of us ladies had the best size for her, we proceeded to show how it was worn. We all postured with the piece of lingerie, cupping our breasts and showing how to use the hooks and eyes in back. Arwilda showed how to hook it in front first and then twist the bra around into the convenient cupping position for appropriate fit. Debra covered her mouth with both hands, while her cheeks turned crimson under her brown skin, and her eyes danced with laughter. I'm afraid the demonstration caused quite a riot among all of us girls in the house. We nearly died of uncontrollable laughter! Our party was almost as enjoyable to everyone in attendance as the bra demonstration had been prior to the big event! Our guests and the male PCV's puzzled at the grins and chuckles our household shared among ourselves throughout the delightful evening. Even quiet, shy Debra, showered us with marvelous flashing smiles every time our eyes met. When her hands were free, she covered her mouth with both of them and we could see her shoulders shake with laughter. The event was extremely successful for everyone!

CHAPTER 14
COPTIC CHURCH TEACHINGS

The shape of the world came up in class one day, and a group of the students challenged me regarding the spheroid on which we live.

"How do you know about this spherical shape?" I was challenged by several young men while the rest of the class looked on with great interest. "Why can we not be on a great flat piece of land surrounded by water with the airplane flying above?" With my limited knowledge of science, I asked of the students that if the Earth were flat, how could our oceans stay in place? Would they not run off the edge of the flat Earth and soon disappear into some void? Evidence of a spherical Earth can be seen by anyone on a shoreline watching for ships to appear. First the tips of the sail, masthead, or smokestacks appear. Then more of the ocean going vessel comes into fuller shape as it approaches over the curvature of the Earth. When one flies in a plane high above, the curve of the Earth can be observable at times, especially when flying over the ocean. The higher one is up, the more of the Earth's "roundness" or curvature is seen.

As I shared my limited knowledge, students softly whispered, "Wonderful, wonderful, wonderful." A few of the students declared their knowledge of gravity, explaining why we did not fall off our planet, and why the waters of the ocean did not fly in a spray off into the atmosphere. Some students squirmed uncomfortably as this was being discussed. I asked if they had other concerns. Finally, Lakech Ali, the bright shining star pupil in class, said, "Madame, our priests have always taught us that the Earth is flat." I'm sure there was a puzzled look on my face when I repeated as a statement that the priests had taught that the Earth was flat. Silently, my class waited for a response. I had heard that many of the priests were not happy that the Emperor has requested Peace Corps teachers to help bring Ethiopia into the twentieth century. Many of us treaded sacred ground when discussing science.

"Perhaps the priests have not had an opportunity to read much about our enormous Earth and the even vaster universe," I said slowly, not wanting to create dissension between these young people eager to devour everything they could learn, and the centuries' old teachings of the learned priests in the church. "Someday, when the younger priests or the children of the older ones return to the church with degrees from colleges and universities around the world, they will help some of the elders to see how exciting new ideas are. For now, it is good to respect the elders' beliefs, and if asked what you are learning, simply state that there is an enormous world that you want to learn more about. Remember, some people will never want to look at anything differently than that with which they were instructed as a youth. Hopefully, educated people will always tolerate different ways of looking at the same thing. Knowing that the world is round or spherical comes through education and experience. Believing that the world is flat, without ever hearing anything or seeing facts to the contrary, is charming and naive, but dear to some. Always be kind and try not to argue with those who have not had the opportunity to learn." My conscience bothered me for sometime after that day. Perhaps I had been a bit too arrogant. I greatly desired my students to learn and question, but at the same time, I wanted them to take pride in their own heritage

A week later the seventh and eighth grade students were assembled in the morning and told that it was a church day. We marched together up the hill to St. Giorgi's Coptic Church, which looked down upon our town of Dessie. This day was Mudhanne Alum, Amharic for "Savior of the World."

We paraded up the hill, four abreast to the church. The first wall we passed through encircled the complete religious compound. On the interior of the circle, mud and grass huts hugged the stone wall. These were the homes of the priests of the church. Since Coptic priests were allowed to marry, wives stood by doors to the dwellings, holding babies on their hips while other young ones ran around. Servants squatted near cooking fires outside the dwellings.

We then passed through the opening of another wall that encircled a perfectly round church. We proceeded to walk around the outside of the church three times, as required to show our respect for the Trinity. Upon the completion of the third walk, we stood in place within the massive circles, which now included worshippers from the town, beggars, leppers, the blind, students and faculty, for the whole student body had joined us now. In the background we heard the deep sound of drums and priests chanting, The resonance echoed over the mountain tops. Some elderly men in our crowd leaned on crude wooden crutches, while others had one wooden pole topped with a carved or ornate metal arm piece for placing under one armpit to lean upon and to shift their weight during the lengthy service. Other people leaned against the stone wall of the compound or squatted on the ground in little clusters. It amazed me how elderly men and women could squat for hours on end, and then stand up an walk off.

Suddenly, a monk in a white loin cloth with a shamma over his shoulders, looking like a wild medicine man, came jumping through the crowd. Worshippers seemed to expect him and cleared a pathway for him. He jumped and whirled around, preaching to the crowd in excited Amharic, waving his arms and pointing fingers. Some of the students near me had bent their heads down and were chuckling. I asked them what had created the humorous reaction from them. They replied that the priest had just said that the Earth stands still and the sun revolves around it. They stated that they had learned quite differently in their science classes.

At this point a whole procession of chanting priests exited the church and began to parade around the outside of the structure three times. They were richly adorned in black or burgundy velvet capes, which were encrusted with sparkling stones, sequins and gold braiding. Many carried velvet or satin umbrellas, which also glittered with decorations. Some wore studded crowns that glittered in the sunlight. They were a splendid sight in this impoverished place.

While most of the villagers looked on with awe, some of the students turned their faces away. When I questioned them about their reactions, they quietly said that the clergy owned much of the land, and they became silent once again. Their silence seemed to say more than additional words might have. The sight of the poor, the beggars, the lepers and the blind, in contrast to this splendor, somewhat repulsed me. Students later said that the clergy could be doing so much more for those with needs, but that when people have much they become too self-centered and greedy. Such wisdom these students already possessed.

A few of the girls asked if I would like to enter the church after the ceremony was over. We went to the women's entrance (discrimination) and took off our shoes as was the custom for all who entered. Most people were barefoot anyway. We entered the outer circle of the main sanctuary and then passed over the threshold into the inner circle. Inside the church were no chairs nor pews. Some rugs were scattered on the floor where some people squatted and prayed. Others simply stood or leaned against walls. Most worshippers appeared to be praying. Tapestries and paintings of the life of Christ, the Virgin Mary and Saint George covered the walls. Many were done in typical Ethiopian art that outlines everyone's eyes in black. Of course, there were also pictures of Emperor Haile Selassie, Empress Woizero Siheen (after whom our school had been named) and Asfa Wosen, the son of the Emperor and Empress. The vividness of the paintings and the portrayals on the walls were quite a contrast to the drabness that we saw in all the homes and buildings here. Most buildings do have a picture of the Emperor adorning the wall in an obvious location.

Both the church and the service reminded me of my exotic location. Although the people appeared to be very devout, many seemed to be uninformed about their own theology. A sweet childlike acceptance of God's love in Christ seemed to be enough to most. People appeared to hold the church service in high regard and many enjoyed the pageantry of it. It was more than just a morning's escape from the regular routine. It was a reminder of God's working in their lives and increased the belief that the Almighty was in charge. There is much to learn from a simple day to day faith of these dear people.

CHAPTER 15
THE GIRLS' CLUB

Ato Yifru Gibayu, our school's headmaster, had suggested to me that a Girls' Club might benefit the nearly two hundred girls enrolled at our school of fourteen hundred students. I had put off the organization of the club until a rather unusual incident occurred.

Walking past my classroom an hour after the school day had ended, I heard some soft voices coming from inside. When I quietly pushed the door open, a group of girls uncomfortably looked up from the desks. Several of the girls had been softly weeping. I asked if I could be of help to them. After an embarrassed silence, one voice replied that I wouldn't understand. A few others shook their head while Lakech, sitting in the shadow, said, "I think we can tell Tshainesh."

There was some awkward shifting and nervous swallows as I entered and sat down in their midst. I quietly waited while some mustered courage to begin. Zuriashwork spoke softly with her head lowered. "We are cursed, Madame" She paused and breathed deeply before continuing. "The blood comes upon us regularly and we are shamed." They all shook their heads yes to this and were embarrassed to look at me.

I gently smiled as I inquired, "You mean, some or all of you have begun to have monthly periods when you pass blood through you bottom?" All of the tear-stained faces jerked up to look at me with open astonishment. I slowly continued, "This is called menstruation and it happens to every female around the world, sometime between the ages of nine and thirteen. I menstruate monthly too. I began when

I was eleven years old. It is part of the process of preparing women to bare children."

"But isn't it wrong, Madame, even sinful. Our parents think the flow of blood means we are no longer pure, not virgins any more. They think the blood flow means we have been with a man. None of us have. We are all good girls. If they discover that we have the flow of blood, they will cast us out. Then we are forced into prostitution to support ourselves. What can we do?"

As the girls poured their hearts out in grief and fear, I listened. They were a support group for each other by bringing together rags, washing them for each other, drying them in the bushes, helping each other during their periods so no family member would find out. Some of the girls knew about sanitary napkins, which were available at the Arab souks, but being single, they would not think about buying them. A family member might find out. Furthermore, most had no money for such purchases. I tried to give them as much reassurance as I could at that moment.

A girls' organization was definitely necessary. When I suggested it, all were eager. They were hungry to know more about these changes in their bodies. To have a safe place to discuss this "normal process" was imperative. Perhaps some of the parents could be educated as well. Puberty should not be a stigma for these girls who were eager to assist each other and should not have to suffer from the ignorance of others.

I went back to my house to write a letter to the Kimberly-Clark Company in Neenah-Menasha, Wisconsin for a copy of the film I had used when teaching sex education to students in Milwaukee. It was called *The Story of Menstruation*. I explained the situation in our mountain village of Ethiopia, and requested a copy of the film

There had been only a two day notice given for the start of the Girls' Club. Two hundred young ladies were at our first meeting, almost every girl at Woizero Siheen School. The purpose of our club was explained to all in attendance . Word had already spread about what had transpired in the classroom after school with the frightened and concerned girls. All appeared to want more information. To defuse some of the anxiety, I taught the group a few camp songs ("Kum Ba Ya," "Old MacDonald Had a Farm," "Row, Row, Row Your Boat," and "Brother John.") The girls had taught me "Brother John" in Amharic, "Wondim Jacob." It was so good to hear the excited chatter of the girls. They acted so American when they were excited. Election of officers would be at the meeting next week. I hoped the elections would go peacefully without too many hurt feelings.

On the way home another girl, a Tigrean, begged me to stop at her home where the birth of a baby was being celebrated. About twenty shammaed women sat in a circle on mats on the floor, eating "gumfu." This special porridge, piled in a bowl, looked like mashed potatoes with a hollow in the center where melted butter and berbere seeped into the mixture. Each person pulled off a scoop of the mixture with the fingers of the right hand, and dipped it into the spicy sauce. Although I did not care for the "gumfu," I enjoyed the warmth and hospitality of the women. These women from Tigre, a province in the north, had their own language, but the law required them to speak in Amharic, the official language of Ethiopia. They were thrilled that I could converse with them in Amharic. I was the first white woman any had ever met.

The Girls' Club elections took place. Everyone wanted Lakech Ali to be the President. This capable and much loved young woman assumed her duties as if born to them. We planned a candle-lighting initiation ceremony that was very impressive. The film on menstruation arrived during our first month of organization. We invited all the female relatives of the girls to attend the viewing. The two Ethiopian women teachers attended as well. They helped with the question and answer portions, so they could explain things clearly in Amharic. Many of the women and girls cried in relief to discover that this was part of nature. No evil spirit had taken possession of them. Some still said that they could never explain this to their parents. They would still have to keep their periods secret. However, they would someday be able to help their own daughters. In the meantime, the girls could all be support for each other.

Although I wrote a thank-you letter to the Kimberly-Clark people, I don't think they could comprehend the impact their film had on two hundred girls and several dozen older females in this Ethiopian village high in the mountains of East Africa.

One day I was out of school with a bad case of diarrhea. Since the one commode at school for males and females did not flush, and feces simply piled up in it with a horrendous smell, my stomach also turned with nausea. I knew two days in bed with a clean bathroom nearby, tea to combat dehydration, and lomotil to control the stomach problem, would help me.

On the first day I was absent from school, a dozen of the girls from our club came to visit me. Their concern for my welfare almost moved me to tears. They were so sympathetic. It seemed as if all the girls in the school knew of my visit to Lakech when she had been ill. I had apparently been the only teacher to ever visit an ill student before. On the second day of my absence, an even greater crowd appeared at my bedroom door. This time some of the male students came as well. It was a bit awkward given the nature of my illness. I was touched by everyone's concern. This time Lakech brought me a huge bunch of bananas and a dozen oranges. She appeared to be thrilled to be giving me something. I felt awful accepting this gift because I knew she only earned ten dollars a month from her tutoring of a child. The fruit must have cost at least her month's salary. On top of it, I knew she really needed the fresh fruit for her health condition. In order to see that she earned more, I asked her for some Amharic reading and writing lessons on Saturday or Sunday afternoons. What an excellent teacher she was. Her shyness dissipated as she worked with me one on one. I stocked her up with apples, oranges, bananas, tangerines, carrots and cabbage. In the package, I slipped some candy, cookies, and several books. The doctor has hope that proper diet will help her since she is young and otherwise, quite healthy.

I had fallen in love with my students. A little meant so very much to them. They were all so extremely easy to engage in conversation. Perhaps more gets taught after school than in class. A number of students walked all of us PCV's home each day, carrying books or sometimes carrying a few groceries, just to continue conversing. Their curiosity, inquisitiveness, and eagerness to learn were so gratifying. They were like sponges, absorbing everything placed before them.

The Girls' Club decided that this year they wanted to be part of the Christmas program put on each year by the school for the whole community. In the past, only the boys put on a play, usually "Romeo and Juliet." The young men were truly a Shakespearean troupe, with the boys playing both male and female parts. The girls decided they wanted to do the traditional Christmas story. They cast the girls who were "orange-hued" as the angels. Girls with darker skin were to be Joseph, the Wisemen, and the shepherds. Gennet, a light-skinned girl, was Mary. Several girls brought animal hides and sheep skins for covering themselves while making appropriate animal noises. A stuffed blanket was the Christ child.

For the fire on the ground while the "shepherds" awaited the host of angels, I brought in a flashlight. When I switched on the light, the girls screamed and jumped back. "How did the light from the stick jump over to the wall? one girl screamed. "It must be magic!" whispered several others. I switched the flashlight off and had each girl experience turning it off and on. We took the flashlight apart to see the batteries and the bulb. The girls were awestruck.

On our final rehearsal, the girls asked if the shepherds could sing while waiting for the angels to appear. Since we had sung at almost every one of our club meetings, and since this was a Christmas pageant, I was in complete agreement. However, I did not think to ask which song they planned on singing. The lights dimmed. The flashlight under a red cloth showed the shepherds sitting around their fire with their sheep bleating softly and the cows lowing. The cast started clapping their hands in unison and singing, "Old MacZonald Haz Ze

Farm, E, I, E, I, O." As they continued their song, the grin on my face grew broader as did the grins on a few other of the PCV's who were assisting. The Americans could refrain from laughter no longer. As we attempted to stifle our laughter, the girls stopped in the middle of the song to ask why we were reacting so strangely to the Christmas story. I finally controlled myself enough to ask why they had selected "Old MacDonald?" Their response was something to the effect that a farmer has sheep and cows. So why wouldn't shepherds, who care for sheep and cattle, sing songs about them? It made sense and was so charming. It had to remain a part of our Christmas pageant. Our school auditorium was packed with town's people who all thoroughly enjoyed the program, especially the animal sounds in "Old MacDonald."

Now, when I list my favorite Christmas carols, some look at me strangely when I head the list with "Old MacDonald Had a Farm."

CHAPTER 16
OUR HOLIDAY CELEBRATIONS

For Thanksgiving, the guys at one of the houses raised two big turkeys for our dinner. The school had given us Thanksgiving Day off. Everyone contributed and we had a feast together: turkey with stuffing, mashed potatoes with gravy, cranberry sauce, carrots and peas, pickles and olives, homemade biscuits with marmalade, fried chicken, fruit salad, pumpkin pie with whipped cream, and tea and coffee. We included many of our Ethiopian friends and colleagues. We had all received our stoves and refrigerators just a day before this holiday. This really helped with our preparations. One of the other fellows had received a stereo phonograph in his trunk. So we listened to and sang along with the music to *Camelot, West Side Story, Harry Belafonte at Carnegie Hall*, etc. We also exchanged names for Christmas presents, and one of the other houses offered to have us all over for that holiday. What a fine Thanksgiving!.

Since the Ethiopian Christmas is celebrated in January, our Head Master gave us our Christmas Day off. We had to return on December 26th. Student examinations began on that day. After several days of examinations provided by the Ministry of Education, the students were to present their holiday assembly, and school would then be closed from January 4th-21st.

I was told Christmas here was quite different: no exchanging of gifts (This was done during the Ethiopian New Year last September.); no Santa Claus; no Christmas trees nor decorations; no cards nor carols., etc. However, to the poor people it is exciting because on

Christmas, even the poor (better than half of the population) have meat to eat.

One Thursday I was invited to the home of one of the Indians on our faculty. Mr. Pakkiam's wife had been eager to meet me. She dressed me in a beautiful sari and I asked her to order one for me from India. She visited my house two days later with her six year old daughter, Indira. I showed her how to smock pillows. Arwilda, one of my housemates, had taught me this. I was making smocked pillows for Christmas gifts. Mrs. Pakkiam then gave me some lessons in making curry, which to this day, is one of my favorite dishes. Indian women were more out-going than the Ethiopian women. This is probably due in part to a better knowledge of English.

In one of my Christmas cards from Milwaukee, I received the exciting news that my old school, Peckham Junior High, might be sending some textbooks for my students. The Peckham Student Council was raising money to ship the books by sea freight. Books are so desperately needed. Students have been studying frantically for their exams from copious notes they have taken in classes. Their future education depends upon their passing the examinations. One can sense the tension mounting as the time nears. On a lighter note, one of my students has become a pen-pal with a student at Peckham. The Peckham student sent him a map of Wisconsin, stamps, and a five page letter.

We, also, were excited at the news that all of the Ethiopian PCV's had a workshop scheduled in the city of Asmara, Eritrea during our break. Eritrea used to be the country bordering Ethiopia to the north on the Red Sea. Some time before we arrived, it had been made into a province of Ethiopia. [Ethiopia and Eritrea fought a bloody war in the eighties for Eritrean independence.] We were told that Asmara was a very beautiful city with many Italian influences since Eritrea had once been occupied by the Italians. Tree-lined boulevards with sidewalk cafes were there. It was a two-day drive from Dessie through beautiful mountainous country. I was looking forward to this experience and to seeing other Peace Corps friends.

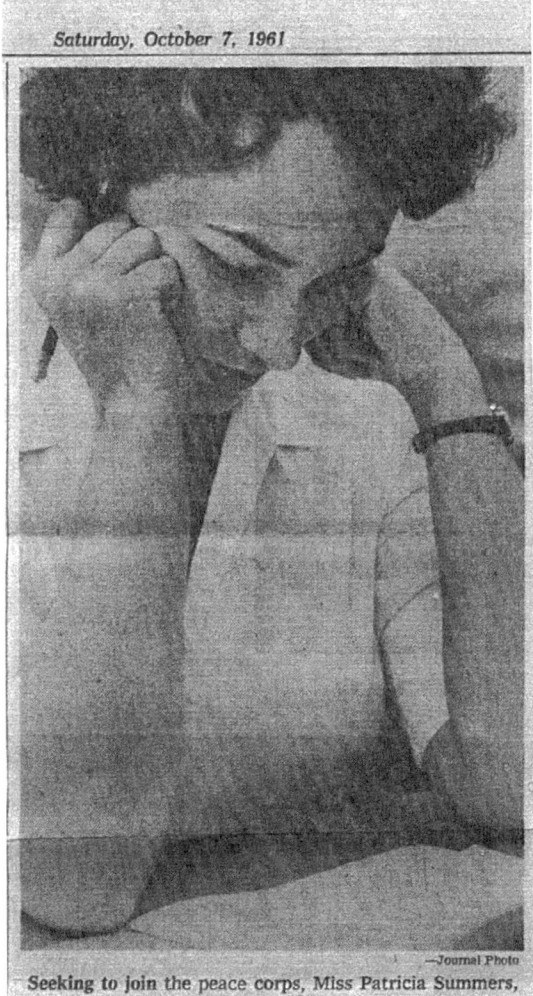

Saturday, October 7, 1961

—Journal Photo

Seeking to join the peace corps, Miss Patricia Summers, 1718 N. 16th st., took a six hour examination Saturday at the federal building, 517 E. Wisconsin av. Ten persons took the tests here. Similar examinations were given Saturday at Ashland, Beloit, Kenosha, La Crosse, Madison, Wausau, Oshkosh, Eau Claire and Green Bay.

Author taking Peace Corps exam (from photo in the *Milwaukee Journal*, Saturday, October 7, 1961)

Top: His Imperial Majesty, Emperor Haile Selassie I, King of Kings, Conquering Lion of the Tribe of Judah

Bottom: Presentation to H.I.M. at Jubilee Palace. Back of author's head. I spoke to him in Amharic. (Harris Wolford, Director of Peace Corps, Africa is on the left.)

Mountainous roads and drop-offs between Addis Abeba and Dessie

Clockwise from top: Donkeys and acacia trees.

Laundry drying on the side of a creek.

People riding on a gherry, it costs 25 cents. Expensive for most people.

Traditional plow with oxen.

Men along the road.

Top left: Neatly filing down to the piazza - the center of Dessie.

Top right: Inhabitants of our town and children from the elementary school take designated spots for celebrations.

Bottom left: We fill the piazza.

Bottom right: A speaker on the balcony of the Telecommunications Building announces our celebration.

Top left: Every school day we line up by class on the field facing the main school building. We recite the flag salute, sing the national anthem, and a Christian and a Muslim lead in prayer.

Top right: Students parade by class down the hill from the main school building.

Bottom left: We exit through the main gate...

Bottom right: ...and pass the newer school.

OUR DESSIE PEACE CORPS GROUP
We made treks to the Danikil Desert. The Danikil women laughed and pointed at the Peace Corps women for wearing clothes above the waist.

On some treks we visited the Boti market in the desert. I even bargained for a camel.

LEPERS ARE GIVEN TRAINING AT THE LEPROSARIUM
Some learn to make looms and weave cloth…
…some learning cooking and cleaning skills.
Others winnow grain or are trained in animal husbandry.

Top: THE DESSIE MARKET
Some people walk two to three days to barter and/or make purchases in the market place.
Note the gallows. People were hung from the gallows in the market for everyone to see.

Bottom, left: Ato Mogus, our "zebunya" or guard, came with the rent we paid on the house.

Bottom, middle: Kebede, our cook, did our shopping after we nearly caused a riot in the market place.

Bottom, right: Deborah, our housekeeper and laundress, had enrolled in 2nd grade.

The family is dressed in wedding finery. Entertainment begins.
Bottom left: Corn-rowing
Bottom right: The bride awaits.

Clockwise from top:

Paulos' family comes to invite me to their home for a visit. (Babo, Solomon are Paul's Christian friends.)

A lady spins with a hand spindle.

Everyone is more relaxed here.

Woizero Fatima is Paulos' mother, 2nd from left. The sister to be married is behind the three children. The children thought I was a ghost because of my white face.

Paul's mother is in doorway. Family and friends watch as I arrive. The cow and its calf was indifferent.

THE WEDDING of Lakech Ali to Kebede Yimam
The family arranged the marriage of 15 year old Lakech to Kebede
who was headmaster of Negus Michael Elementary School.

VISTORS

Sergeant Shriver, who was President Kennedy's brother-in-law, had been appointed to head the Peace Corps. He visited our school with Harris Wofford, who was head of the Peace Corps in Africa.

FACULTY OF
WOIZERO SIHEEN
TIMHERTE BET (Faculty
of Woizero Siheen
Secondary School) 1964
Pat and Bob wearing
y'ager libs, the national
dress of the country.

Top: We meet Frehiwot Kebede,
Lakech's daughter.
Middle: Frehiwot gives Pat Wollo
province women's clothing.
Bottom: Kebede Yimam was
Lakech Ali's husband and the
father of Frehiwot Kebede.
Kebede was imprisoned over
11 years because he had served in
the Ministry of Education under a
previous ruling party. Kebede is
on the left, Pat and
Dr. Frehiwot Kebede.

In between preparing students for their exams, each Peace Corps house had been putting up a little Christmas tree and working on homemade presents. My satin smocked pillows were coming along. It was fortunate that we were so busy. It kept us from dwelling too much on the holidays. We had all been trying to cheer each other up. This was the first time any of us had been away from home at Christmas. At our house we strung popcorn and made some ornaments out of silver paper we had collected. We also made chains out of some colored paper. We bought socks, books, and candy for the boys we were sponsoring and wrapped their gifts. The boys were thrilled. to see packages under the tree for them. I took five of my knee socks and filled them with fruit and candy for my housemates. They were surprised on Christmas morning.

Sunday evening twelve of us caroled at the homes of Indian teachers on our faculty who were Christians. We enjoyed ourselves and it put us in a Christmas spirit. Afterwards we went to the home of one of the groups of fellows for egg-nogg and popcorn. We played several rounds of charades. Monday the 24th we taught all day and were invited for tea at one of the Indian homes after school. The Sudan Interior Mission people invited us Christmas Eve, and the Lutheran Mission in Dessie invited us for Christmas Day.

Fifteen of our group packed themselves into our two Jeeps for Christmas Eve at the Leprosarium. We first caroled for the lepers. We returned to the home of one of the missionaries and continued singing. Mr. Jones, the head of the station gave an excellent Christmas message. These S.I.M. people always made everyone feel so welcome. After the meditation, we had refreshments: pizza; all kinds of crackers and spreads; tons of different homemade cookies and candy; homemade popcorn balls; cocoa and coffee. What a treat! A number of us presented our homemade gifts to our S.I.M. friends

We returned to our village and all of us stopped at one of the Peace Corps houses for our gift exchange. Here was a little tree all decorated. We had cake and coffee while we opened our gifts to each other. Next came the inevitable round of charades. Boy, we were getting good at this game! The gift I received was a lovely set of Ethiopian ankle bracelets. One of the household of fellows confessed the next day that they almost burned their house down. They had wanted to light up their tree and so had placed candles on it. They had only left the room for a short time when someone smelled smoke. Rushing into the room they found the tree on fire and flames going up the wall! Buckets of water extinguished the conflagration, but they had a number of repairs to make as a result.

Christmas Day we all slept in. Ten of us went to the home of the Lutheran missionaries for a one o'clock dinner. Turkey, stuffing, mashed potatoes, gravy, cranberries, carrots, green beans, relishes, and hot apple pie with ice-cream was served. All afternoon we munched on Christmas cookies and drank tea. Then we played—you guessed it—charades!

I now own half of a horse! Arwilda and I decided we wanted one. It was not meant to have anything to do with Christmas, but the purchase came just at this time. We've named it "Kokebe" which means "star." The horse was brown with a white "star' marking on its forehead. We paid $65 Ethiopian for it, which is about $27 American dollars. I don't know how to ride it yet, but I'll learn. Several others have bought horses as well. The students who live with us will take care of them. They were thrilled when we said they could ride them too. A horse is more practical than a car because there are no roads to most of the villages—only pathways.

The Saturday after Christmas, our faculty had a party for all of us. Our faculty now consists of two South Africans, eight Indians, twenty-six Ethiopians, and nineteen PCV's. We were served dishes from each of their countries, and learned songs and dances from them. It was a delightful party.

Most of us have had our fill of celebrations, but at noon on December 31st, we received a visit from a Dr. Spossovitch, a Yugoslavian doctor who worked at the government hospital here in Dessie. He invited our household of ladies to a New Year's Eve party.

We accepted out of curiosity. My little knowledge of Russian along with our Amharic made it possible to communicate with him. The evening was rather boring. The doctor had several other Yugoslavian men there and they all drank heavily. The girls from our house sat on one side of the room and drank Coca Cola and Fanta. Very few words were exchanged with the host. We left before midnight.

The examinations were now over. All had been graded. Over seventy per cent of my students had passed. That was very high for here. Only one student had passed the semester before we came. Lakech Ali had the highest passing grade with a 91%, and this with also having the lead in the Christmas play. She was such an avid student and delightful person. However, she brought me some rather sad news that she told me in strictest confidence. Her sisters were arranging a marriage for her. Lakech was upset to the point of tears. Her heart's desire was to have an education and to someday choose her own husband. She appeared to hope that I could do something. Her family only spoke Amharic. My knowledge was not extensive enough to discuss this with them. Lakech also explained that since her family was so poor, they seemed to feel that they would be able to make a good match for her because her knowledge of English speaking, reading and writing would provide a good dowry for her in obtaining a husband of higher status. She did not know of any husband who would allow a wife to remain in school. My heart was heavy for her as she shared this unhappy information. She wanted me to know this before I left on the Asmara trip. I took her hands in mine and softy asked if there was anything I could do. With eyes downcast she replied that she had to be obedient to her family and do as they requested. She promised to tell me more when school began again after our break.

I felt such sorrow as I watched her walk stoop-shouldered away. What could I do? Perhaps there was some sympathetic Ethiopian woman who could make Lakech's case to her family. Most girls in this culture are married by thirteen or fourteen. Lakech was fifteen. I had read of these dilemmas in novels; here was one facing us in real life.

Perhaps sharing Lakech's dilemma with individuals during our up-coming Asmara trip, especially PC friends from other locales in Ethiopia, I might develop some suggestions for my favorite student.

CHAPTER 17
ASMARA TRIP

Our house was a crash pad for many PCV's making their trip north to Asmara. I had to remain in Dessie a day longer than most since our Christmas play was on the seventh of January. Cora, from Washington, D.C., also decided to wait. We were driving to Asmara with George, Marc, Gene, and Jerry. Almost everyone else had left this morning. We've given our cook time off until everyone gets back, so I was hoping to experiment with cooking. Batches of sugar cookies, oatmeal cookies, biscuits, and cinnamon sweet rolls, along with carrots and onions browned in butter and sugar with potatoes, made up our meals for the day. Meat was not available due to a time of fasting. I had really begun to enjoy cooking when I had the time. Our kerosene stove was still difficult to control and very dirty.

The day's hectic ness was compounded by one of our students fracturing his arm while riding one of the horses. I took him to the hospital, and had to wait for a doctor who could help set the bone. Never a dull moment!

Cora and I had taken a two day vacation at Boro Meda before leaving for Asmara with the guys. We were offered a guest cottage to stay, relax and unwind after the busy exam schedule, Christmas play, and feeding so many PCV's on their way to the meetings up north. Those missionaries were always so gracious to feed and house us when they work hard themselves with all the lepers, over 200 patients in the Leprosarium and an equal number coming daily from the countryside for treatment. About ten trachoma operations on eyes were done daily, as I mentioned previously.

I helped Helen Estelle, the wife of one of the missionaries, bake. She had insisted on sending along lunch for all six of us for our two day ride. They promised to pray for our safety since there are shiftas—armed bandits—who hold up cars by placing piles of rocks in the road to make vehicles stop. Then they steal everything the can see. The road itself should be interesting with 21 hair-pin turns in one area. Sounds dizzying! The shiftas lived in the mountains ranges near Asmara. They were active after dark. We will leave early and be watchful.

After a midnight rising and early breakfast, we loaded the car and began our long ride. We were determined to make the trip in one day. The moon was full and extremely bright. It lit up the beautiful mountain roads and bathed the valleys in light. I feasted on the awesome beauty of the peaceful, sleeping villages, consisting of groups of three to ten grass huts. I was stunned by the charm the moonlight gave to them. As the sun began to rise, we reached the foot of the mountains and ahead of us stretched the sandy and rocky plains of Alamata. The huts on these plains were of stone and mud. No trees could be seen for miles around. We drove all day, eating chicken and donuts made by Gene, and the potato salad, sandwiches and cookies I had made with Estelle. The only incident along the way was a flat tire, which was easily changed. As we neared the Eritrean border, we began climbing again into the mountains over roads with many hair pin turns and drop-offs of thousands of feet. It was getting dark—time for shifta activity. We had to reach Asmara before the sun went down behind the mountains, to avoid the shiftas. We finally saw the lights of a big city.

Asmara, the beautiful city with boulevards, shops, and restaurants, was quite a sight after Dessie and even Addis Abeba. It was the most modern city in Ethiopia, looking very European. The main streets were lined with palm trees. There was a huge downtown area with many nice shops. There were window displays in most of the store fronts. There were even cinemas. People dressed in the latest fashions, so that we, PCV's, felt almost out of place with our white tennis shoes. There were many beautiful Italian villas and charming little narrow streets. The mosques and array of lovely wild flowers everywhere, gave us a definite flavor of the Middle East. The ladies stayed in a lovely, three story villa overlooking Asmara. The floors were marble. On the second level was a sunning patio onto which the bedrooms opened. Poinsettias flourished in large pots on the sunny deck. Steps led down to another patio and garden. Here doors led to a hall for the downstairs. There was HOT running water in both the kitchen and the bath. Sheer luxury! This was the home of four female Peace Corps teachers in Asmara. I was delighted to find that the villa was Carolyn Wood's house. Carolyn had been my roommate in Peace Corps training at Georgetown. It was great to see her.

There was a big U.S. Military base in Asmara called Kagnew Station One evening we went there to see an American film, *Cowboy*, with Jack Lemmon. We also bought some Butterfingers, Milky Ways, and Oh Henry candy bars. They were great! We returned to Kagnew several times and had glorious hamburgers with fresh lettuce and tomatoes—pure ambrosia! We also had ice cream! The drive was worth these two things alone! The meetings were rather innocuous, but seeing friends, sharing experiences, and visiting this city was fabulous.

Jerry, Gene and I decided to take the three hour drive to the beach city of Massawa on the Red Sea. The drive was almost *straight* down, for we drop from 7000 feet to sea-level. As a result, there was a noticeable change in temperature—from forty degrees to ninety degrees! On the drive down there were 81 hair pin turns! Jerry wanted to collect some shell specimens for his classes.

Massawa was the largest of the two seaports in the province of Eritrea. The other seaport was Assab. Massawa, a small town with a very Middle Eastern influence, was surrounded by very arid and barren terrain. Only a few palm trees clumped together here and there. Camel caravans loaded with exotic paraphernalia swayed across the desert on their way to market places. Few people were seen on the streets because of the intense sun and heat. The buildings were made of clay bricks. We were told that this was the hottest seaport city in the world, with temperatures up to 150 degrees. Summer averages 135 degrees! We were happy to drive back up to cool Asmara.

After a series of Peace Corps meetings and some shopping in the marvelous stores, Jean and Don excitedly told our Dessie crew about a ship which was supposed to dock in Massawa and sail south to the other seaport of Assab. They thought it would be interesting to try to sign on as deck passengers and then take the bus from Assab back to Dessie. Ten of us became quite excited. We got a good night's sleep, packed as few things as possible in one of the jeeps, loaded excess in the jeep left in Asmara, and ten of us took off for Massawa.

In Massawa we immediately went to shipping companies. However, to our disappointment, there was no ship leaving for Assab that day. One was expected in a day or two. We looked over our finances and discovered that we probably would not have enough money for a hotel if we were to spend money on a ship's passage and a bus ticket.

We then had a brilliant idea. Off shore from Massawa was an island. We could sleep on the beach there for free. This would cost nothing other than a few cents for a boat to the island, some bread, cheese, and oranges for nourishment, and drinking water. From the island we could see if the ship came in.

It was easy to hire a boat with an awning for just a few dollars to take the ten of us to the island. We made it clear that we were to be picked up early the next morning. The island was called Green Island and it was quite beautiful. Waves lap the shoreline and exotic birds dive for delicacies in the warm water. One half of the island was sandy beach and the other half was thick bush. In the center were ruins of several big buildings. Some said that the buildings were part of Mussolini's summer home. Others said they were part of a base for the Italian army. Whatever they were, they were interesting to explore. After our explorations, we swam near the shore. Some collected shells and other specimens to take back to classes in Dessie. We gathered drift wood and made a big bonfire on the beach. After our meal of bread, cheese and oranges, we sang a few songs. and spread towels on the sun-warmed sand for sleeping.

As we began to doze, we were startled wide awake from Jean's frightened scream. A rat had just run over her! We stopped to listen and heard the squealing of hundreds of rodents coming from the tall grasses. The island must have been infested with them. We moved as close to the water as we could to keep from getting wet when the tide came in. We hoped the rats wouldn't be interested in coming that close to the water. We built the fire between ourselves and the rats. Periodically we turned on our flashlights. We gasped at the dozens of pairs of eyes staring back at us. Throughout the night we took turns tossing wood on the fire and catching some sleep. The early part of the night was very dark. Later the moon came up and somehow, the rats stopped bothering us. At sun-up no big ship had arrived in port.

While we sat on the beach in the morning, waiting for our boat to return, we looked across to Massawa, a beige sleepy town with its minarets arising from several mosques. Mountain ranges flung themselves to over 7000 feet above this town which was located at sea level. Some of us would need to climb the winding mountainous road to return to Asmara and drive our jeep back to Dessie. We drew straws to see who would do this. The shortest two ends fell to Marc and George. They said they would leave as soon as we returned to Massawa.

Along the beaches on the shoreline across the way, were clumps of palm trees and people walking alongside of/or riding on camels in the sand. A few huts were located near the trees. Beneath the clear waters of the Red Sea much aquatic life could be seen. Beautiful coral and millions of different shell fish were visible. However, we were told that it wasn't too safe to do a lot of swimming because of sharks and sting rays, We washed our faces in the salty Red Sea and waited for our boat to take us back to the mainland.

Our boat finally arrived and returned us to Massawa, a typical Middle Eastern town with sand coming right up to all the reddish-beige mud buildings. Colonnades shaded the front of the main string of shops. Tables and chairs were placed in the shaded colonaded areas, inviting customers to stop for coffee or tea and to catch some sea breezes. Drinking something hot when it was hot outside, we were told, equalized the heat inside and outside so that one was more comfortable. I found this to be true. To our disappointment, no ship had arrived. The man at the shipping company said, "Maybe tomorrow." Well, we couldn't take another night on the island and we couldn't afford hotels, so we were considering riding on the literina, or train, back to Asmaa at noon. While we were sitting in the shade of a colonnade, all feeling very dejected, Don happened to look out at the harbor. Somehow we all noticed the change in his facial expression. We all looked out to the harbor and there was a BEAUTIFUL ship heading into port. We jumped up and let out whoops! We could have been heard all the way to Asmara!

Arwilda, Don and I managed to get on board the Lena Christine Brodin. The floors were carpeted, the mahogany woodwork gleamed from polishing, and the inside was air conditioned! We persuaded the Captain of the Swedish cargo liner to let a group of us buy deck passage. We were all becoming low on funds so we bargained a good price of $35.00 Ethiopian each ($14.00 U.S.). The Captain and crew were most gracious, serving us sumptuous meals, giving us air-conditioned cabins, and showing a Yul Brenner and Deborah Kerr film, *The Journey*, in the evening. We had only asked to be deck passengers since the ride was about eighteen hours, but we were treated like royalty, and for thirty-five dollars Ethi. per person! Even with a beautiful cabin waiting for me, I was too excited to go to sleep. I went out on the deck to the very front of the ship. Here the wind was strong but balmy. The sound of the wind and the waves was so loud.

As I stood there, right in front of the ship the moon rose above the horizon. The ship seemed to sail right into its moonlit path. My formerly impossible dreams of seeing exotic places were again a reality! I will long remember my ride on the Lena Christina Brodin, the Captain and his crew!

The next part of our adventure was a little less thrilling, but a lot more challenging. When we disembarked, there were customs' officials everywhere who wanted to inspect our purses. They walked us for what seemed like miles, to a custom's house. After we sat for an hour, and numerous officials had inspected our few belongings, gawking at us all the while, they decided to let us go on our way.

Assab was a very small port. One could walk through it in a half hour. It was very barren with only a few trees. Everywhere was sand. Occasional Arab traders with their camels could be seen. Narrow streets, a few mosques, and several shops made up the town. We had very little money left, and hoped we could hitch a ride on a lorry. However, lorrys didn't get to this town too often. Most of us were flat broke by this time. A kind gentleman in town let us sleep at his little pension, free. Fortunately, the next morning, Bob and Irene Embrey, a Peace Corps couple from Dessie, were able to get some money from a little bank in town so we could all get bus tickets.

A bus ride in Ethiopia was unlike any bus ride we had ever had in the U.S. The bus seats were very close together so that one's knees became blistered from the back of the seat in front. In addition, people often sat three to a seat. Fortunately it was a Saturday and the bus was not crowded with goats, sheep, and hens. In fact, for the first part of the trip, the bus was not crowded at all. We were the only "ferengis" on the bus. The others were a motley assortment of Ethiopians in business suits, and Danikil warriors with enormous bushy hair-do's, and who wore long wrap-around skirts and carried long spears or swords.

The major portion of the ride was across the barren, dry, dusty Danikil Desert. Along the road were camel caravans, herds of goats, gazelle, and oxen. In one place an ostrich leaped out in front of the bus and ran ahead of us for about five kilometers. Ostriches run at fantastic speeds of sixty to seventy miles an hour. We cheered the bird on with hoots and hollers! It was wonderful to watch. The bus made a hundred stops at least! At every "tukel" or "sar-bet" and even where there was just open space! It stopped for people to urinate, and it stopped for lunches. If people got sick, they just stuck their heads out the windows that were all open. Pity the people in the rear of the bus. The bus stopped four times for custom's inspection, although nothing was really inspected. We had left at six in the morning and arrived in Dessie at ten at night.

What an experience this whole trip was! I am in love with Ethiopia and can not devour enough of this wonderful area of the world.

CHAPTER 18
GIRLS' CLUB UNIFORMS AND
"Y'AGER LIBS" OR
"CLOTHES OF THE COUNTRY"

I was informed that our school's supply room had received several hundred beige women's skirts. Perhaps the Girl's Club could incorporate them into some kind of uniform. Upon investigation of the boxes, it was discovered that all the skirts were size 14. "Not to worry," replied the girls. "We all sew." So a skirt was distributed to each of the young ladies, much to the consternation of the supply room's "zebunya" or guard. This overseer of school texts, pencils, and composition books went berserk when consumable materials were taken out of his sight. However, he could do little but grumble over the skirts since our headmaster had issued the order.

At our next meeting, all 150 girls arrived in the beige skirts which had been tailored to their tiny frames, for most teen-age girls in Ethiopia are quite petite. The majority were wearing white blouses with sweaters or a "natala," a white, gauzy shawl worn by females. They were excited to have their "uniforms" because Parents' Day was eminent. Parents' Day this year arrived on the same day as a government holiday which commemorated the victory of the Battle of Adua. The day also happened to be a Saturday. Many more parents would be available to attend. In the morning, classes were held so parents could come to see us teach and to visit our classrooms. Students had decorated our rooms with many colorful wild flowers.

Numerous visitors came to the room. They seemed to enjoy themselves and were eager to hear me use my meager Amharic vocabulary.

The afternoon consisted of a gymnastic performance, a scout performance, a music performance under the direction of P.C.V's, Ron Bell and Otto Rink, and a debate. I was asked to give a short speech in Amharic about the Girls' Club. My young ladies, properly attired in their "uniforms," cheered as did the crowd. It was the first time a foreigner had ever given a talk in Amharic in their town. People kept coming all afternoon to thank me for speaking in their language! They said they understood every word. Little did they know how long I had practiced that speech, with Lakech's help. Although I had shared several alternatives to her engagement, she repeated her need to comply with her sisters' wishes. "A good girl must listen to her family," she insisted. My "uniformed" girls circulated through the crowd selling our school newspaper and refreshments. An exhibition of handicrafts followed the other festivities. I bought some crochet work, bookends, and basketry.

Skip and Helen Estelle with their four children from the S.I.M. Mission had come for the Parents' Day festivities. Afterwards they drove me to Cambolsha, 20 Kkllometers down the mountain road from Dessie. We had a delicious dinner there at a lovely, clean, Italian restaurant and hotel. After our meal we were too exhausted to attend the play that was being given that night at the school. I also declined their kind invitation to come with them and stay overnight at the mission. I had already promised two students that I would walk with them to the mission in the morning to attend church, a 2-2 ½ hour walk to Boro Meda! I was a glutton for punishment, but a promise is a promise!

Sunday morning's walk was glorious. Solomon and Babo from my Bible class at the Lutheran Mission, were promptly early. They knew a short-cut to the S.I.M. Mission, so it only took us 1 hour and 45 minutes to get there. Our invigorating, early morning walk took us past many beautiful fields with animals grazing. Ethiopians were busily hurrying along paths. Sar-bets (grass huts) nestled on hillsides and in eucalyptus groves. Huge rock formations dotted much of the countryside. During the walk the boys entertained me with folk tales of the area. It was a delightful walk, and we arrived at the mission five minutes before the morning service. After the service, I lunched with Beryl and Shirley, the two missionary nurses. The boys lunched with some of their Ethiopian acquaintances. We visited for the afternoon and Helen drove the boys and me back home. I was given some fresh rhubarb. When I got home, I cooked it with some sugar and served it to my house-mates. It tasted very refreshing.

Because of our successful Parents' Day, our Headmaster gave everyone Monday off. Our Dessie crew piled into the jeeps and headed down the mountain to Bati, a little town in the Danakil Desert. Although we had been there before, we were always fascinated by the herds of camel, and the market place. Women usually led the family camel loaded with bent twigs, animal skins, and all of the other family belongings. They were the ones who set up the hut at the end of the daily migration looking for watering places for any of their livestock. That day the desert was very hot and we were getting sun burnt. The place reeked of rancid butter, which was used to plait hair. We made our way back up the mountain.

The next day Arwilda and I decided to get fitted for "y'ager libs" or clothes of the country. Most clothing was made on a street directly off the piazza, where many store fronts displayed men sewing industriously on old Singer sewing machines, feet pushing away at the pedal and hands guiding material as needles rapidly pounded up and down making neat seams. We first selected beautiful bordered patterns on the endless meters of white gauze-like material. Once purchased, we were measured and told to return the next day. Our purchases of the National Dress of Ethiopia fit us perfectly. They were fairly snug in the midriff. This is probably because most Ethiopian women do not possess bras. In fact, few have even heard of bras. We began to wear the National Dress to many celebrations and special events. The villagers and our students loved to see us clothed in the country's garb. My girls wanted to corn-row my hair, but I never had the courage for that. George Parish, in the Peace Corps house across the street, also had "y'ager libs" made for him as did Cora Morehead. I think George was the only male PCV to have this done.

Since my little speech at the Parents' Day program, people have been stopping me on the street to talk. Little do they know that I had practiced those words over and over again for a whole week. It was difficult to explain to them that my vocabulary was still quite limited.

Four of my girl students had heard that I had walked to Boro Meda with Babo and Solomon. They insisted that they had to accompany me to the Leprosarium. Our walk took almost three hours. They were much slower walkers and talked incessantly, typical of girls almost anywhere in the world. Upon our arrival Helen Estelle served an American dinner for them. Since Easter was coming, the girls were fasting and couldn't eat meat or any animal product such as milk or butter. Helen was aware of this from the kitchens of the 200 leppers who resided on the compound. She had prepared all kinds of vegetables, bread and strawberry jam, and jell-o with fruit. The vegetables were quite bland for the girls since Ethiopians eat very spicy fare. However, they loved the wiggly jell-o and the jam and bread. Beryl Johnson showed the girls the hospital and lepper colony. Two of the students were interested in becoming nurses. Helen showed the girls her eight month old baby boy, a perfect specimen of a healthy baby, chubby and always smiling. The girls were amazed at how strong the baby was. Many Ethiopian babies were very frail. Most families experienced 3 to 6 infant deaths before a child reached age five. If an infant could survive for five years, it was pretty certain to grow up. The girls were delighted with their experience.

The following weekend the PC fellows across the street invited all of the PCV's in town and all the SIM missionaries for a picnic lunch and bar-b-q. Everyone came and we feasted on bar-b-q chicken, baked beans, potato salad, deviled eggs, hot garlic bread, cucumber salad, pineapple upside-down cake and colas. We played volleyball and badminton, sang and talked. Hundreds of turkey vultures sat in the tops of the trees watching us consume our food. When we threw a piece of meat in the air, they would swoop down and catch it in flight! We decided to tie a piece of meat on a long string to see what would happen. Holding onto the end of the string, one of the fellows threw the meat into the air. A vulture caught it and started to fly off only to discover the meat was attached to the string. The bird flew in circles on the end of the line, eating the meat off the end. One time toilet paper was attached to the string too. It was rather humorous watching the bird take off in the breeze with the toilet paper waving behind. We discovered all kinds of creative amusements.

My Girls' Club soon had another opportunity to dress in their uniforms, and for Arwilda, Cora and me to wear the national dress. The occasion was a battalion of United Nations forces who had fought in the Congo would parade through Dessie with a real band. The girls made an enormous floral wreath to welcome them. The U. N. soldiers looked smart in their military garb with their light blue helmets. This was the first real parade since I had left home. The whole town flooded the piazza to enjoy the spectacle.

CHAPTER 19
STUDENT HIKES AND VISITATIONS

One day I took my 8th grade English classes on a picnic in the mountains that tower over Dessie. While we were planning the picnic, the girls in class said that they would not be able to go. So during the week, when school was over, I visited the homes of all the girls to convince their parents to allow their daughters this opportunity. At each home the parents served some Ethiopian dish. The visits were very pleasant and they all agreed to let the girls join with the whole class on our outing. Gene Rosachi, one of the PCV's across the street, asked to join with us.

The fifteen mile hike which went over rocky terrain did not always have trails. We clambered to the top of one mountain area where we came upon a mineral spring near a very large tree which spread its branches parallel to the ground but just above our heads, providing a lot of shade. A stone wall encircled the spring and many bottles with putrid contents lined the wall. The students said that many superstitious people considered the spring to have magical properties. People with stomach ailments would drink from the spring. The mineral water would help them to vomit what was problematic internally. The vomit was put in the bottles as a type of offering to the sacred well and tree. As a result, these people believed that the well contained magical properties, and they worshipped both the well and the large tree nearby. At least, this was told to us by our students. We explained to our students that mineral water was sold in the States to aid people there with upset stomachs. We told them that we didn't attribute magical powers to it. We just know mineral water can be very helpful for a number if stomach problems.

We continued to climb to another outcropping where we were able to have a panoramic view of Dessie far below us. After the plateau we went straight down for awhile and then began to climb again. This time, when we arrived at the top, we saw hundreds of monkeys. We also came upon the remains of an Italian fort, left from the Italian occupation of Ethiopia. It was nearing lunch time, so we started looking for a mountain stream. We went to the other side of the mountain and a beautiful meadow stretched out on the floor of the valley. The students wanted to go down there because they said that there were streams in this area. We began our descent and soon the trail disappeared once again and we were slipping and sliding down the side of the mountain. In one place we came upon a thicket of thorny acacia bushes and we nearly had to crawl on our hands and knees to pass through the area. We finally got to the bottom, but, much to our disappointment, there was no stream. We continued around the mountain and suddenly came upon a tukul and cultivated fields. Alongside was a little stream. We filled the metal pots we had carried, built a fire and boiled the water for nearly an hour. Everyone was happy for the rest period. It was also a great time to share English-Amharic vocabulary words for use in our writing about the day's experiences. We were finally able to make tea that was poured into the plastic cups we had also brought along. We ate rolls and hard candy.

The woman, who lived in the tukul nearby, invited Gene and me to come in for coffee and some hard-boiled eggs, a real delicacy in this country. The tukul or sar-bet (grass house) was very practical. Upon entering the round grass hut, there was an outer ring around the wall where the animals were kept. Then in the center were the living quarters for the family. The outer circle housed the lambs, a calf, a horse and chickens so that they were safe at night from hyenas and other predators. The body heat of the animals inside also provided warmth for the human inhabitants.

After our rest, one of the lady's children showed us a short-cut back to Dessie. Within two hours, a straggling bunch of exhausted students and teachers arrived in the town. Some of the boys' adrenalin was still surging from our encounter with six hyenas. They had shown their bravery by chasing, hollering and waving their arms at the predators! Our large group alone would have been enough to scare them away!

After church on Sunday one of my other 8th grade boys had asked me to visit his home. I had passed it last Sunday while walking to Boro Meda. Although I was still stiff from Saturday's hike and picnic, my curiosity and my promise to visit convinced me to go. After lunch, I proceeded with Paulos and Solomon to Paulos' house. Paul's family are Muslims, but Paul was on his way to becoming a Christian. His family had originally named him Mohammed, but they have accepted his name change with indifference. Before ascending the mountain path where Paul's home was located, we explored the large rocks at the bottom of the trail. The boys told a legend that went along with the rocks. It was about a bride and groom and their horse being changed into stone. We continued to climb the hillside where a beautiful trail led us to the top. Along the sides of the trail were many other tukuls. Finally we arrived at Paul's home. His mother greeted us warmly, inviting us inside and serving roasted whole ears of corn, boiled milk, and "dabbo," a type of bread. She roasted coffee beans over the fire on the floor of the tukul. I offered to crush the beans in the wooden container with a mallet for pounding them to powder. It was an interesting procedure. All the while we visited and ate, people from miles around the area kept popping their heads into the hut. I greeted them all in Amharic, and many would giggle or cover their faces. As my eyes became adjusted to the darkness inside, I saw a cow with her calf in the outer ring of the circle. Outside I took many pictures. Fatima, Paul's 13 year old sister was to be married in 20 days. I was asked to please return for the wedding.

Upon our return to Dessie, we stopped at the Lutheran Youth Hostel where Paul stayed. We played Dominos. The Hostel's youth director invited us to stay for a meal of injerra and wat. The meal was followed by the singing of many Gospel songs, and we had fun harmonizing. The evening ended with a radio Gospel broadcast

As I walked the short distance back to my house, I again basked in the delight of another challenging, exhausting but wonderful weekend. I just wish I could get some of my house mates to come with me. I had been inviting them to join me. I was so glad that Gene had gone on the Saturday hike and picnic. Most of the Peace Corps enjoyed the visits to Boro Meda, American meals, and the friendliness of the missionaries there. However, many seem to have drawn a line in socializing with students. Several had become friends with some of the Ethiopian teachers. That seemed to be good. I think the ladies in my house think I am weird. I enjoy being with them, but I can be with Americans anytime. I received numerous invitations weekly to visit in homes. The curiosity of the Ethiopians to learn about America, about me, about my family, appeared to equal my curiosity about these gracious people. They are so tolerant and patient with my slaughtering of their language. Perhaps they appreciate my attempts. I wanted to absorb as much as possible while I was here.

CHAPTER 20
FUNERALS AND POLITICS

I have never been to nor seen so many funerals as here in Ethiopia. Weekly, sometimes twice a week, we saw and heard funeral processions winding their way up the mountainside on the road in front of our school. A very rocky, but wide, dirt road rose off the piazza in the center of Dessie. The road wound behind the Telecommunications Building which houses the one Post Office in town. The piazza was at the bottom of this hilly, rocky road, where many coffee and tea shops, as well as other tiny souks, were located. A third of the way up this stony dirt road, and veering to the left, was a tall iron gate set into square stone columns. Behind the gate was another steep dirt road leading up to the old stone structure of the main building of Woizero Siheen Secondary School with its many detached classrooms and newer two storey building. The school compound sat on a mesa overlooking the piazza and the back of the Telecommunications Building.

As one continued up the main dirt road in front of our school compound, St. Giogis Coptic Church was reached at the top. This was the destination of funeral processions that were filled with black clothed, weeping, wailing mourners, who carried the black cloth-covered pallet of the recently deceased. Some mourners carried large framed portraits of the loved one. Some of the framed portraits were attached to the backs of donkeys. The love for the individual was often demonstrated by the number and noise level of the mourners.

It was not unusual to hear of students and younger children dying of simple things like dysentery. There were many cases of lung diseases like TB and pneumonia. The extremely high death rate among babies and young mothers was appalling.

We had not attended any of the funerals until we heard, in March of our first year, that Ras Gabrehiwot, a man of 95 years of age (a fantastic age for anyone in this country) had died. He had been loved by many in Dessie as well as respected by people throughout the entire empire. The title "Ras" is much like the title "Sir" as bestowed upon people in high favor by the Queen of England. Haile Selassie had bestowed this honor on Gabrehiwot.

Here I must digress into some history of the country. Before the 18th Century the thirteen provinces of Ethiopia each had its own king. This had been the type of rule throughout the country's history. However, in the middle of the 1800's, Theodros, a usurper, assumed power and united all the provinces and kingdoms of Ethiopia. He was the first to do so. After his death there were a few years of confusion until Menelik II took the throne and established unity of the provinces. After his death around 1913, a queen, Zoditu, ruled for about 2 or 3 years. Others tried to become Emperor but the country again fell into disunity until a young man by the name of Ras Trafari Makonnen, began to gain more and more power. He was able to subdue all the kings of the provinces and establish himself as King of Kings, or Negus Negast, Haile Selassie. His full title was Emperor Haile Selassie I, King of Kings, Conquering Lion of the Tribe of Judah, His Imperial Majesty. He set up rule in Shoa Province at the city of Addis Abeba.

In the Province of Wollo where Dessie is the largest city, lived Negus Michael, the most powerful of all the kings of the provinces. Although Selassie had subdued all the kings, he had to keep them in favor as well. Negus Michael still exerted much power. As a result, Selassie made his own son, Crown Prince Asfa Wossen, governor of Wollo Province. Then he made Negus Michael's son, Gebrehiwot, a Ras. Ras Gabrehiwot was also the brother of Woizero Siheen, after whom our school had been named.

We heard, as we made our ascent to school that Emperor Haile Selassie, himself, would be coming to Dessie for the funeral!

The whole town immediately went into mourning. Men and women clothed themselves in black. Some of the poorer dressed in sackcloth, took stones and scratched the skin off their cheeks. Then they threw ashes over their heads in mourning demonstrations. When we arrived in the center of town to climb the hill to school that day, the piazza was jammed with mobs of mourners. The weeping and wailing rose to the heavens.

As usual, the students were lined up on the school field for the morning flag raising ceremony and prayer. Our Head Master came forward and announced that His Imperial Majesty was on his way to Dessie along with the Crown Prince and other officials to attend the funeral. I was to organize the Girls' Club for the funeral procession, and other PCV's were to make a floral arrangement. We were sent home to change into black. The girls put on their beige skirts and wore black sweaters or black mourning shawls. We all grouped together and followed the hysterical river of mourners up the steep, rocky hill to St. Giorgis Church. Numerous mourners carried framed pictures of the Ras. Even the large paintings were draped in black. Many wailed while some in sackcloth danced mourning dances.

Upon entering the church compound, we saw lines of priests dressed in splendid black or maroon robes, which were encrusted with sequined designs that glittered in the sunlight. On their heads many wore hats with crown-like decorations that also glittered. Other priests wore the traditional black or white headpiece. They carried ornately colorful umbrellas also covered with sequined designs, which sparkled in the bright sunlight. They chanted and sang, accompanied by large mournful drums and tinkling bells. What a spectacular sight they were. I'm sure many of the poor in attendance came just to see this colorful spectacle, as well as to get a glimpse of their Emperor.

All around the church compound danced mourners with bleeding faces which had been torn by the rocks in their hands or their fingernails.

We heard that the Emperor's plane had arrived at the emergency landing field in Cambolsha, the town 20 kilometers down the mountain. The thousands of mourners in the church compound tried to move into any area of shade they could find. The sun was intensely hot and shade was very scarce. We all waited in the hot sun for three hours. Finally, after nearly melting in the sun, we saw a stream of cars draped with black cloths being ushered into the compound by armed guards. The weeping and wailing intensified. Arms waved in the air and all kinds of mourning demonstrations increased to a frenzied fervor with the arrival of His Majesty. Soldiers swarmed all over as His Imperial Majesty exited his vehicle and ascended the steps of the church, followed by the Crown Prince and other officials. The royal party stopped on the top step, turned and faced the crowd. Even His Majesty was weeping. We were surprised by the show of emotionalism from the highest on down to the peasant. It was explained to us that this beloved Ras had distributed hundreds of acres of his own land to many of the poor people. In addition, his last son had died just the previous week. With the Ras's death today, the last of the royal family of Wollo Province had passed away. To the older generation, the tradition that they loved and to which they had clung, had passed away with the death of this Ras.

I looked around at the faces of the students in this enormous gathering. They, like us, were there because it was a school requirement. Their interest, like ours, appeared to be curiosity. In contrast were the thousands of mourning adults. To me they seemed to be grieving for more than the death of a great and beloved individual. They grieved also for the gradual passing of an era of tradition to which they had clung for assurance and familiarity. The public expression of grief seemed to be such an extremely emotional and yet natural experience to these people. Even the soldiers seemed to be helpless to control the crowds and their own emotions as they, too, wept.

I felt very privileged to be in Dessie today. This was a most rare experience. To observe this portion of Ethiopian history gave me a further glimpse into the character and personality of these dear people. Each insight helped me to understand a little more the importance of the past and the role of tradition in their lives. In some ways they appeared to be a nation of little children, blindly following their leader.

Many students and those with higher education had expressed to some of the PCV's their unhappiness with H.I.M. They felt it was time for him to start sharing power. Selassie was becoming old. Who or what would replace him? Too many people had not been educated and communication was so poor throughout the empire. There were still tribes who did not recognize or even know about the Emperor. Many worried that when Selassie was gone would his successor be one with whom the West could work?

> *Dear Mom,*
>
> *All my thoughts and experiences here in Ethiopia, I have been writing in these detailed letters that I know you are keeping and organizing for me. I hope I am writing vividly enough so you can picture situations and events here. Actually, I feel as if I am having more interesting experiences than most of the PCV's. I have been invited to so many homes and family events. This is partly due to knowing more Amharic than the other Americans, and partly due to spending much time with the students. I frequently invite others to join me on these visits to families of students. Students have discovered that I don't look with distain upon their simple huts, and that I enjoy conversing with their "uneducated families." I really think I am learning more from these people than I can ever give to them.*

By the way, thank you for writing to the students from whom you have received letters. They are so proud to show your letters to others. This shouldn't become a problem for you with the arrival of dozens of correspondence from my students! That won't happen. Few have enough money to afford paper and pencil, let alone a stamp! A few students are corresponding with some of my former Peckham Junior High School students. They have been exchanging photos and postcards. Students here eagerly share their correspondence from American with others.

I have so little to offer these eager students other than my time spent with them, and the time seems to be going very rapidly.

Wouldn't Dad have loved to hear of all my adventures?

Give my love to all.

Your studious daughter

CHAPTER 21
MUSLIM FRIENDS
AND THEIR CELEBRATIONS

Many of the shops or souks in Dessie were owned by Arabs who followed their Muslim traditions. Several mosques were in town with their minarets towering above shops and the piazza. Others dotted the countryside. Several times a day we heard the muezzins chanting from the tops of minarets as the faithful were called to prayer.

The Muslim holiday, Ramadan, was celebrated in the month of January during our first year in Ethiopia. The holiday lasted a full month. During this time all faithful Muslims fasted from early morning until evening. In fact, they couldn't even swallow their own saliva. My first encounter with this was when several students began to spit on the classroom floor. In order to keep my classroom as sanitary as possible, I rearranged the seating so that all my Muslim students sat near the windows so they could spit outside. They were very cooperative and careful to expectorate out the window.

In the evening families often feasted. One day during the holiday, I was invited to accompany Lakech Ali to the home of a wealthy Indian woman who was Muslim. The married woman had four children. I watched her prepare the evening feast. We went through the house and out the back door where a mud house with no doors, opened to a little courtyard. This place was used for most of the cooking. On the floor of the mud house were stones arranged so two cooking fires could accommodate several pots. In one pot she was cooking lamb in a very spicy curry and pepper sauce. Over the other fire simmered other foods in oil. One was a type of dough, called "gaugul" which was dipped in syrup made of sugar after it was cooked. It was very sweet but tasty, somewhat like a donut. Another food was a tart with meat, onions, and pepper inside. Still another was a spicy round bun made of grains I had never heard about before. There was also a type of pudding with ginger and cinnamon. I was then served the complete meal. It was delicious. The preparations were most engrossing. The woman must have used the whole day to mix and prepare the many dishes. Our hostess invited me to return and to bring the other Peace Corps ladies. I hoped my housemates would want to accompany me next time. The villagers loved having me over and I thoroughly enjoyed every one of these visits. It made the whole Peace Corps experience more meaningful to me.

On the last day of Ramadan, all of our Muslim students were excused from school. After school the woman whom I had visited with Lakech, invited all of the American ladies to her home to celebrate the end of the festival. I discovered that the name of the woman was Woizero Rahema. We all went and tasted the many exotic foods. Again, the woman had gone to so much effort for us to enjoy her holiday. I felt somewhat uncomfortable with my countrywomen. They made little attempt to communicate with our hostess. Instead they only talked among themselves and picked at the food, showing little interest in being there. I appreciated Carolyn's smiles shared with the woman. I was concerned that some of our PCV's were too indifferent to being here. Perhaps I was the odd one. Or perhaps that was how some Americans would conduct themselves in jobs back in the U.S. Maybe I was just too "gung-ho" as my brothers Bob and Russ would say from their Marine Corps background. Whatever it was, I was having a BLAST!

One day I invited two Muslim married couples over for dinner. The day was spent in preparing for it. Our cook had to buy Muslim meat and our chickens had to be slaughtered by a pure Muslim. Our cook prepared four different kinds of Ethiopian wat. I made Jell-o salad, cucumbers and tomatoes in sweet-sour sauce, and a carrot-raisin salad. I also baked cookies. The two couples who came were Woizero Rahema and her husband, and a 14 year old Arab bride, Woizero Zeneb, with her husband. Woizero Rahema was the Indian lady whose home we visited at Ramadan. I had also previously visited the home of Zeneb, who was so lonely as a new bride. She told me that she often felt like a prisoner in her own home. She wanted me to teach her how to smock pillows the way Arwilda had taught me.

The couples were thrilled with the invitation to our home and enjoyed all the food, especially the Jell-o with fruit. Woizero Rahema's husband spoke some English, but the others knew none. I showed them pictures from Wisconsin that Mom had sent to me. Some of my housemates also shared photos of the U.S. Our guests were surprised that we would eat Muslim meat. I said that God had created all animals and it made no difference to me who did the slaughtering. My housemates really seemed to enjoy our guests and said that they might go visiting more often with me. During this visit we were not allowed to have any of the Peace Corps males over while the Muslim women were in our home. This would be against Muslim law. Both women had arrived covered in veils and left the same way. Because Rahema and Zeneb were distantly related, both of the husbands could be present at this invitation. We all learned to adjust to new customs.

I had been invited to Paulos Assen's 13 year old sister's wedding. It was a Muslim wedding in the countryside. Gene Rosachi, from the Peace Corps house across the street, asked to join me.

Here was another glimpse into the culture. The bride had never seen the groom. She would first see him on her wedding night. Friends of the groom's family helped find a suitable bride. Then the groom, in secret, had a glimpse of the girl to decide if he wanted her for a bride. Once he agreed to his bride, a friend of the groom signed a marriage contract with the girl's parents. The wedding date was set. On the day of the wedding, the bride's family, relatives and neighbors celebrated all day long with feasting, drinking, dancing, and music. The girl was moved into a separate sar-bet (grass hut) where all the children came and entertained her with songs and dances. The bride was usually almost a child herself. Her female friends visited with her. Later in the day, the friend of the bridegroom came with a dowry. The groom NEVER attended the festivities; neither did his family. However, since people knew the American teachers would be present at this countryside wedding, the family did attend—but not the groom. The friend of the bridegroom went with the bride's mother to the bride's hut to present the dowry to her. The dowry was usually clothing. The women formed a circle around the girl while she tried on the different pieces of clothing. The friend of the groom and others formed a circle outside, near the door of the hut, where they sang, danced and drank barley wine (tala).

After the girl had tried on the last dress, she was completely covered in a shamma (a large shawl) so no part of her could be seen. Then she was carried on the back of a male relative with the mother leading the way. Both mother and the completely covered daughter, sat on the ground while all the women present, formed a circle around them, singing and clapping. The mother lifted part of the daughter's covering to cut her child's nails and shave portions of her hair. Then once again the bride was carried "piggy-back" to her hut. The celebrating continued. Later in the evening, the friend of the groom would carry the bride off to her husband, much like a thief snatching someone away. It all seemed quite primitive.

We were received as honored guests. Paulos was concerned that since we were Christians, we wouldn't eat the Muslim meat at the festivities. Once again I explained why it made no difference. I was invited into the bride's hut where the girls tried to teach me the various songs and dances. A huge metal barrel served as a drum. I was invited to join in beating on it. Paulos and his family thanked Gene and me for coming to the celebration. The countryside around the Assen family would probably share for many years the time two white Westerners attended a wedding in their area.

The Arab shopkeepers were always very accommodating. I bought some candles at one of the shops in town just as a deluge of rain began. I didn't have my umbrella with me and I had a three kilometer walk home. The owner of the shop loaned me an umbrella! I was quite astonished. His kindness changed the concept I had had of Arab traders. In another Arab shop where I bought some material for making culottes, the owner gave me matching thread. They all appeared to be very fair with us. Perhaps we're finally coming to be accepted by the whole town.

One day three females, dressed in purdah, black robes from head to toe, stopped at my door and asked if I would comes for tea at their compound. They said that they were the wives of one of the Arab shop owners. We set a day and time for a visit. When I arrived at the high, fenced-in compound, I knocked on the gate in the wall. The door was opened and a voice from behind it requested me to come in. As the door was shut, I was amazed to see four beautiful young ladies dressed in lovely European suits and wearing black pumps on their feet. They said the youngest was 13 and the oldest 20. They giggled and covered their faces, then asked me to be seated in an upholstered chair. Three of the wives sat down on a couch while the other one called at the door for a servant to bring in refreshments. Hot sweet tea steamed in glasses. Dishes of dates and nuts appeared along with plates of various sweets and tinned cookies. As they plied me with delicacies, they also asked rather humorous questions. "Is it true that women in America shave their legs and their armpits? Why?" I explained how this shaving of hair was usually done for personal hygiene.

I was asked, "Is it true that men have only one wife? How terrible!" They explained that Muslim men could have up to four wives, but only if he could afford to treat them equally. The wives in most harems became closer than sisters and selected different tasks in the household, they explained. The one who loved to cook supervised the shopping and the kitchen. The one who loved to clean supervised the laundry and the household. The one who loved children supervised their up-bringing and education. The one who loved the bedroom, was most frequently available to the husband. No one had to do everything. Life in America must be very difficult for women! They made some very interesting points! Then the girls brought out a Sears-Roebuck catalogue. They said that they often ordered from it. Was it true that hosiery now came with panties? Their own legs were bare, but they wanted to place an order. Servants brought in 6 little ones for me to see. The youngest was only two months old. Of course, I was asked if I was married and/or had children. This was asked all the time. Whenever I made my reply of "no" there were always sad little clucking noises made. I was well past the marriageable age, according to the customs of Ethiopia! This is a country that believed in marriage, and the earlier the better!

After my visit to this "harem," the Arab shop keepers seemed to be even more eager to stock the shelves of their souks with items the Americans liked — Toblerone candy bars, tins of cookies, and jars of jam.

I didn't recall seeing any animosity among the Muslim community, Coptic Church community, nor the animistic groups of people during our two years in the country. Perhaps, I was too much of a "Pollyana" and tended to see the positive aspects of everything in life. I hoped I hadn't lost too much objectivity in my writing as a result.

CHAPTER 22
SUMMER VACATION: A WEDDING, OUR PROJECT, AND EGYPT

Our first school year here in Dessie, Ethiopia, had ended. Yesterday was the presentation of awards to all the students with the highest marks in their class. It was almost humorous to see all the city officials sitting on the small stage while tall and short, young and old, male and female, barefooted and shoed, crossed the stage to get an award from the provincial governor. All the schools in Wollo province, including the priests' schools, had students receiving awards.

Lakech had received three awards. Over the months since her announcement of the betrothal arranged by her sisters, we had tried to see if any alternatives were possible. Kebede Yimam, the headmaster of Negus Michael Elementary School in town, was her betrothed. He came to visit me declaring his deep love for Lakech. He promised that she could continue her schooling even if there was a child. A wet nurse would be hired to nurse any baby. Kebede knew that his bride-to-be was an outstanding student and he loved her all the more because of this. Lakech could definitely continue her education. Almost weekly the engaged couple came to visit me. Each time Kebede declared his love for Lakech and reiterated his desire for her to continue her schooling. The wedding was to be the Sunday after school was out. He had even ordered a white wedding gown from Asmara for his Bride. All of the Peace Corps teachers were invited to the wedding and the following celebration.

On Sunday I was told to be at St. Giorgi Coptic Church at 6:00 AM. The bride and groom had to be there at 3:00 AM. When I arrived, I was taken into the inner part of the church after leaving my shoes outside, as is the custom. Inside the bride and groom were clothed together in one long, black cape with a gold-sequined collar. They each wore interesting headpieces. I was allowed to take pictures. After hours of praying, singing, chanting and swinging of incense, the wedding party remained with the priests until early afternoon. At noon, I was told to return around 3:00 in the afternoon with other PCV's. At that time, our jeep joined in the wedding car caravan and drove through the town honking horns, much like here in the U.S. We then drove out into the countryside to a grassy meadow where everyone formed groups for wedding pictures. From this caravan we returned to town where a wedding tent had been erected. Long tables of food abounded and a group played Ethiopian instruments and sang. Raw meat, a delicacy, was passed around with a hot berbere sauce. Servers hacked off pieces of the raw meat from a pole on which the carcass was draped. They tried to reassure us that the berbere killed any bacteria in the raw meat. We said thank you but our stomachs were too sensitive.

I had gone to the reception with George Parish. Both of us had summer projects that were to begin early Monday morning so we had wanted to excuse ourselves in the early evening. Lakech didn't want me to leave. She clung to my hand and burst into tears. She fell into my arms crying. I felt so badly for her. In some ways I felt almost like her mother. I had been told that her mother was in an institution for the insane. Her sisters were not in attendance. There was no one to give her any advice or comfort. My heart went out to this fifteen year old girl whose marriage had been arranged, even though I felt her husband was sincerely kind and cared deeply for her. I felt so helpless and inadequate. I tried to reassure her by reminding her of the words Kebede had shared at my house, of his undying love for her and that she would still be continuing with her schooling in fall. I told her that I was praying for happiness for both of them.

Monday began our projects.

The Peace Corps had encouraged all volunteers to commit themselves to some project for part of our summer vacation. The other portion of the summer we could travel anywhere on the continent of Africa. We could NOT, however, leave this area of the world.

George and Marc Clausen had chosen an agricultural project. They had already experimented with growing popping corn. Since Ethiopian corn is quite stunted, they had tried a comparison of several rows of American corn with the native Ethiopian corn. As they expected, the American corn grew rapidly and tall. The shorter Ethiopian corn was stunted in its growth, but continued to grow. One day the fellows looked at the rows of corn and saw tiny caterpillars all over the rows. Within a day the American corn was consumed by the pests, but the native corn still continued to grow. This was quite a learning experiment.

Their new summer project had actually begun before school was out. They had ordered Rhode Island Red chicken eggs. They were now going to build incubators for them. Ethiopian chickens were very scrawny and laid very small eggs. The hope was that the healthier chickens would produce larger eggs and larger birds. They did not want any unfortunate situation to occur as with the corn. Fortunately, they did succeed with this project.

Most of our group selected to help build a school at the SIM Leprosarium. PCV's Ron Bell, David Hurst, John Bigelow, Don Kilhefner, Gene Rosachi, Jerry Lemmert, Jean Boetcher, Carolyn Mulford, Arwilda Bryant and I had heard that a school building was needed at the mission station of Boro Meda. All of us had benefited from the generous giving of the missionaries there. Numerous meals, piles of fresh produce for our homes, overnight visits in the guest homes, and holiday celebrations with these people had helped us to enjoy a bit of the Western world while teaching in Ethiopia. Our summer project would be to help build a school for the leppers. Most of our work would take place during the warm rainy season. We left

Dessie at 7:00 AM daily and returned home around 6:30 or 7:00 PM thoroughly worn out. With the help of the missionaries, the fellows surveyed, measured and strung lines for the building's foundation. The foundation was dug and we all lugged rocks and mud to the trenches. We chopped down saplings for poles. I chopped down three trees by myself! My hands were covered with blisters and every muscle in my body ached. The work was physically exhausting. Many of the male lepper patients helped. The work was *very* different from teaching. I would hate to do this for a living! Most days we came home, washed up, and collapsed into our beds. We were too tired to even have dinner. After the first two weeks we became acclimated to the physical work at this altitude. The foundation was the most difficult. The framing became easier. We learned how to construct walls and sling mud at them! There would be mud walls separating the rooms. We hoped to finish the building before we left on our vacation. The windows and doors would probably have to wait until we returned from our trips.

Our favorite times of the day were the tea breaks in the morning and afternoon, and the wonderful lunches prepared by the missionary ladies! Some days we baked cookies and brought them with us for everyone to share.

One of my best friends from Georgetown training, Cindy Tse, came to spend a month with me in Dessie during this time. Cindy is from San Francisco. Her project was to write a book on Amharic music. She was working with Otto Rink, a PCV here in Dessie. It was so good to have her here. She went to church with me. We cooked and baked together, shared concerns, sang and laughed. We had fun harmonizing. We also became quite excited as we discussed and shared books about Egypt. We planned to be roommates on our trip to that exotic place.

A number of overnight visitors—a group of missionary women, PCV girls exploring the country, and others ladies from Europe—had been stopping at our house for a day or two all during this time. Many were Americans or Europeans traveling across Africa. They always

141

entertained us with wonderful tales and whetted our appetites for our own travels.

I could hardly believe that I would be going to Egypt in a few weeks! It seemed too fantastic. I remembered teaching about ancient Egypt at Peckham Junior High in Milwaukee. To actually see the pyramids, sphinxes, and Sahara Desert up close and personal seemed like a dream. The PCV group going to Egypt had to go to Addis one weekend during our project, to get our passports and visas for Egypt and the Sudan. Our group consisted of Jean Boetcher, Arwilda Bryant, Cindy Tse, David Hurst, Don Kilhefner and me.

Our itinerary for the Egypt trip was to drive from Dessie to Asmara. From there we would fly to Cairo. We planned to spend several days in Cairo exploring the pyramids of Giza, visiting museums and going out to the pyramid at Sakara. From Cairo we would go to Alexandria and spend a few days relaxing on the beach and swimming in the Mediterranean. We also planned to see the Rosetta Stone, which had been used for translating hieroglyphics. The Stone's location was near this city. Our itinerary next called for a train ride south to Thebes, Luxor and Karnak. From there we would take a side trip to Aswan to see the construction of this huge dam. Just south of the dam, we were going to take the Nile Steamer down the River, past Abu Simbal to Wadi Haifa in the Sudan. On the way we expected to see ancient ruins, many of which, like Abu Simbal, would be inundated by the flood waters of the Nile River once the Aswan Dam was completed. From Wadi Haifa we hoped to go by bus to Khartoum, the capital of Sudan. We wanted to visit the ancient city of Omdurman. Then we would fly back into Ethiopia. We planned to carry sleeping bags and duffle bags—no suitcases. It would be cheaper to travel this way. We knew we would probably look like messes, but what an adventure!

The missionaries at the Leprosarium had asked us to take some things to the SIM in Addis when we went for our passports and visas. We arrived early in the morning at the mission headquarters. The people at this SIM insisted on serving us all a huge American breakfast. Mission headquarters was thrilled that the Dessie PCV's had volunteered to build the school at the Leprosarium. These SIM people were so warm towards everyone. Many times I heard the PCV's say that their negative impressions of missionaries had been greatly altered by their encounters with the SIM people.

The summer rains had arrived in the form of monsoons. The full force of the deluge raged all night long. However, the sun shone brightly during the day. We sank in mud while we worked on the school building. But usually by noon, the sun had dried the land enough to make work pleasant.

The roof at our school now covered two of the rooms. It was good to be at this point in the construction because the rains now came 12 out of 24 hours. Sometimes the rain was so heavy we couldn't see out the window. Fortunately, most of the rain still came at night. However, the grounds continued to be so muddy we were working in mud up to our knees in the morning. The altitude and the hot noon sun dried the ground surprisingly fast. We weren't sure we could get the flooring into the building before our trip.

We discovered that our landlord had been over-charging the Peace Corps on our house. We decided to look for a new place to live, since our two year contract could be broken at the end of the first year, upon a sixty day notice. Our landlord, who was charging $380 Ethiopian dollars a month, had forgotten about the clause. Some of the PCV's tried to argue him down the other day, but got no where. Today in our house hunting, we found a charming house for only $200 a month. Arwilda and I went back to our landlord and gave him sixty day notice. After much weeping, wailing, and arguing by Ato Zerufael, our landlord, he finally asked us how much we thought would be a good price on the house. We said $250, which is still $50 too high. Zerufael finally gave in at $280, one hundred dollars cheaper a month than we had been paying. All the while he suggested lower rental prices, I sat sewing and smiling, saying little. I felt like Madame LaFarge in

Dicken's *Tale of Two Cities*! We finally renewed the contract at $280. However, we planned to move into the other house and leave the one we had been occupying for the new group of PCV's who were to arrive in October. Eighteen nurses, doctors and other medical personnel were coming to work in the government hospital here in Dessie. We planned to move into our new quarters upon our return from Egypt.

CHAPTER 23
HYENA IN THE KITCHEN

We arrived back in Ethiopia in September after a month of travel. Cindy, my roommate in Egypt, and I stayed for several days with two other PCV's who were stationed in Tesenai, near Asmara. They too were near a mission station only it was located in a very arid region of western Eritrea. The land was flat and dotted with acacia trees, which we often called "umbrella trees" because of the way the limbs reached out like an opened umbrella, giving shade to those who were beneath it. The grass houses of the missionaries had small matching grass huts out back. These were covered with bright yellow flowers. Inside, a commode covered a hole in the ground. A cabinet, where a basin and pitcher of water had been placed, stood against the mud wall. Towels and soap had been placed near the basin. These were very charming "out houses." We also visited one of the PCV schools. The building was made of saplings which were several inches apart so any circulating breezes could enter unimpeded. A skinny flagpole stood in front of the school house. The fellows in Tesenai took us to see an enormous baobob tree which, from a distance, looked as if the tree were growing upside down. The top tree portion looked like roots extending themselves into the sky. The trunk was so enormous that Cindy and I could stand inside of it, walk around and look out on the arid desert.

At last we bade farewell to our hosts and returned to Asmara where I also had to leave Cindy. I had had a wonderful two months with her. We both had to return to our assignments.

I arrived at the Dessie bus station and Don Kilhefner was there to pick me up. He had returned to our village right after our trip to Egypt. Everyone at my house was already packed and eager to move into our new residence. We were also eager to share our summer adventures, for a number of the others had gone south to Kenya, Tanganyika, Zanzibar, and Uganda. However, our immediate task was to vacate our home for the next groups of PCV's who were to arrive shortly. We were also eager to get ourselves settled in our new quarters.

The new house was on a larger gated compound. A screened-in porch faced the main road. I was glad to see this porch for the boxes of books from Peckham had arrived and their pile filled a good portion of the screened in area. Fortunately the porch could be locked. All of our rooms were very large. However, our living room/dining area opened to a courtyard. We had to go down an open breeze-way to get to the kitchen and storage rooms. Across the courtyard were the rooms for the students who lived with us. The house itself was quite old and made of chica, mud and grass mixed together. It had been painted. We had running water in the bath with a little charcoal water heater, but there was no running water in the kitchen. Also the bedrooms near the kitchen had no glass in the windows, only shutters. The rooms became very cold. One big appeal of the house was all the privacy. The entire compound was completely surrounded by trees of all kinds and flowers abounded. A disadvantage to the house was that it was very far from our school. It took us 45 minutes to walk to Woizero Siheen from this new location. We probably should have thought this through before we decided to move. The final event that made our decision to move AGAIN, was when Arwilda got up in the middle of the night to get a drink of water from the filter in the kitchen. We all were startled from our sleep when we heard her scream. All of us, including the students went running to the kitchen as a huge hyena leaped from the table in the middle of the kitchen floor and ran past all of us as we were arriving at the doorway. I'm not sure who was frightened the most, Arwilda, all of us, or the hyena! We knew we would again have to change our dwelling.

Our original household of ladies was also breaking up. Cora had been transferred to another town where she would be training teachers. Jean wanted to live on her own. Arwilda, Carolyn and I planned to find another place closer to our school and without hyenas visiting us!

As soon as school began, we announced to students to come to our house before we moved, to select books for themselves. We didn't want to have to move the books, too. All the books were in English. Most were hard bound. I later learned that all of Peckham Junior High in Milwaukee had undertaken this project. The most difficult part they had had was raising funds for mailing four hundred books. Even sea freight was expensive. They also sent a set of thirty dictionaries. The students had even included several hundred pencils, pens and writing paper!

When the Ethiopian students saw the pile of books, they gasped in surprise. Most had never seen hard-bound books, only paper or cloth-bound ones. As each made a selection for a book to keep, I was moved by many of their comments. Almost no one had ever had a book of his own. Many held the book to their heart with great wonder. "Madame," they would say, "these are the key to the world." . They sensed that education was a doorway to self improvement. We wrote many letters of appreciation back to Peckham Junior High School, and sent some photos as well. There are very few American students who value their education as deeply as these young people here in Ethiopia.

The new group of 2 doctors, 6 nurses, 3 lab technicians, 3 community health workers, 1 public health nurse, and 3 health educators finally arrived. Four new teachers also came with them. We now have quite an American Community in Dessie. We've all been working hard to get them settled in their houses, and to help them find servants. We held a party at our new, and soon to be old, abode, to welcome the new group and to get to know one another. The provincial governor invited all of us to a cocktail party and reception at his palace. I met his wife who invited me to visit her on Tuesday after school. There have been many invitations to the homes of my Ethiopian friends. They wanted to welcome me back after the vacation. Two of the new PCV's went to church with me. They seemed so young, but it sure was nice to have some Americans with me.

> *Mom,*
>
> *I'm so glad that the wall hanging made by Lakech arrived in Milwaukee. Your initials were embroidered on it along with Lakech's. I thought it was so cute how she signed the card "Mr and Mrs Kebede." Here, the titles "Mr. and Mrs." are not used. Instead a married couple would be called "Ato Kebede and Woizero Lakech." The only change in name when a female is married is from "Woizerit Lakech" to "Woizero Lakech." It was also thoughtful of her husband to make the card for you. He is a fine and bright young man, only 21 years old. I have grown very fond of this young couple. I believe Lakech may be expecting a baby. Kebede is still in total agreement with Lakech about returning to school, even if she is pregnant.*
>
> *Your adventurous daughter*

We finally signed the contract for our new [third] home. This house, as so many in our town, was owned by the Crown Prince. I dealt with his negotiator. A lot of old furniture was left in the house, all in need of repair. But the walls were neatly painted. I made curtains, repaired and painted furniture, and trained a new houseboy who had been taught to cook by the missionaries. We moved to our new home as the new school year started.

It appeared that many of the new PCV's came expecting too much from a developing nation. They thought the country was terribly dirty. They were appalled by the shabby grass homes Ethiopians "actually lived in," and were disgusted by public urination. I don't know what they expected, but they must have missed something in Peace Corps training. One in their group has already returned to the States. The others seemed to have an awful lot of time on their hands. They played Bridge during the day and organized parties in the evenings to expend their energy. Our teaching group wondered if we chose the wrong profession. We were exhausted and had papers to correct from a busy day with our students.

The final results of the year end examinations had finally been posted. Twenty-eight out of 213, who took the eighth grade Ministry Exam failed. This was very good results because usually only 28 pass.

I was again teaching eighth grade English. I had all new students. I hoped I enjoy them as much as last year's young people.

****

Arwilda, Carolyn and I had a few problems with our new house. The comodes leaked and went to an open cesspool outside the bathroom window. The kitchen sink did not work. I had no electricity in my room, and there was only a wood stove to cook on. Otherwise, things were pretty good. We each had our own bedroom. We were now a 10 minute walk from school. We were across the road from the home of Marc, George, Jerry and Gene. They took sympathy on us and invited us for many meals.

We heard that we were to receive a kerosene stove and refrigerator.

****

Yea! They came! Now we have a refrigerator and a stove. I took the wooden crate that the refrigerator came in and turned it into a wardrobe. George came over from across the street to help me hang a rod on which to place clothes hangers in the closet. I sewed a drape for the front and had material left over for matching scarves on my trunks in the room. We were feeling more comfortable in our new home every day. Our house boy was a very good cook. He even knew how to make chocolate cake! We were now inviting the fellows from across the street for meals since they had taken such good care of us during our time of hardship.

****

Carolyn went out to Boro Meda with me several times to stay for the weekend. A number of the new PCV's have also gone to the Leprosarium for Sunday evening services. A few of the newcomers enjoyed singing. One of the girls, Liz, was very good on the little electric organ. Ron Bell appeared to be sweet on her. He joined all of us in singing Inter-Varsity hymns. We had great sing-a-longs.

****

There have been no more hyenas in anyone's kitchen!

CHAPTER 24
TRACHOMA, FLIES,
FLYWHISKS, AND FLEAS

Flies! Flies! Flies! Everywhere we went flies buzzed around our heads. I already wrote about swallowing a fly in Chapter 9. It was not uncommon to see flies clustered around the eyes of little children. Students were more conscientious to brush the flies away. Many carried horse-tail flywhisks or small leaf-covered branches to flick the pests away. Any well-dressed Ethiopian male, garbed in his Y'ger Libs, the white national dress, would usually have his flywhisk in hand to complete his outfit. The whisk is a definite necessity.

Those pesky little flies create a more ominous threat—trachoma! Here is how the problem was explained to me. The fly lays eggs under the eyelids of its victim. The eyelid begins to turn under and the eye lashes rub against the cornea of the eye. After a period of time, the cornea is so irritated that blindness results. We had seen so many blind along the streets. I hadn't realized that many of these afflictions could have been caused by flies. We were also told that trachoma was extremely contagious. An afflicted child who rubs his eyes and then touches anything can pass on the problem to others.

To try to control trachoma outbreaks, a Trachoma Clinic was held at the school and specially trained medical technicians from the Ethiopian Ministry of Health examined every student in the dresser's [nurses] station at the school. Teachers were then told to separate those with trachoma from those without the problem. In my classrooms there were only six without the affliction. I grouped them together in one part of the room. In the meantime, those with trachoma were identified in two separate groups: those who only needed ointment for healing, and those who needed an operation for advanced disease in order to prevent blindness.

Some students returned to class with an obvious layer of ointment around the eyes. This was repeated several days of the week. Others went through a rather uncomfortable surgery. A portion of the eyelid above the eyelashes had to be surgically removed. The remaining skin on the eyelid was then sewn together. To allow the lid to heal, the eyelashes were taped above the eye near the eyebrow. Thus the eye was forced to remain open during healing. A type of patch was worn over the eye which, during healing, had no lid to cover the eye. Some had to have this procedure repeated for both eyes. For a week we saw students being treated to prevent blindness caused by flies. The Trachoma Team remained in our town until all students had been treated.

This was quite a vivid lesson to all of us.

Our own experience with flies bordered on the ridiculous. We couldn't believe the sluggishness of the flies that incessantly buzzed around us. They would sit on us or on furnishings and never move. We had no trouble swatting them. It's just that they were in the billions. When some of us Peace Corps teachers stopped at a "buna bet" or coffee shop near the piazza after school, we would have fly killing contests. These sluggish insects walked slowly all around our table. They would try to balance on the lips of the glasses from which we drank our coffee or tea. We would brush them off our drinks and they would awkwardly topple onto the table. Then we would flick them, with some forceful finger dexterity, at the glasses from which we had just emptied our coffee or tea. The force of the flick would cause the fly to hit strongly against the glass and fall dead on the table. We counted to see who had killed the most flies on the table. John Bigelow had the most dead insects in front of him so he was the champion fly killer, although Don or David was often a runner-up. We laughed at how desperate we had become for entertainment! Later we were able to find the old-fashioned sticky fly paper to hang up in our homes. Some of us also put up screens in our windows to help alleviate the problem. Our other bane during our time in this country was fleas. They too were everywhere! They danced all over us. Many of us bought cans of flea powder at the Arab souks. I sprinkled the powder generously on my bed before putting the sheets on it. Then I sprinkled more on the sheets. I didn't want to be disturbed by these pests at night. During the day we would try to catch them and snap them in half. That was the only sure way we knew of killing them. When we snapped them in half, we could see how much of a blood donation we had just given.

One of the new doctors, who had just arrived in Dessie, loved to hike. However, she had been scratching a flea bite on her leg. Her constant scratching of the bite, created a septic leg. With little care for the leg and constant hiking, her leg became so infected, she had to be airlifted to a hospital in Germany. Many of us thought that as a physician she should have known better. Sometimes people are determined to do what they want no matter what the consequences are.

My favorite flea story, however, took place in Addis. I had become friends with a woman I met at the SIM headquarters in the capital city. Her name was June Bruce and she worked for US-AID. She allowed me to use her APO mailing address so my family could mail me packages inexpensively. This way I could avoid paying bribes at the post office in Dessie when packages arrived from the U.S. June would notify me whenever a package had arrived, and I would arrange to go on the next jeep trip to Addis for the usual group supplies or doctor check-ups. I was also fortunate to be able to stay in her lovely apartment whenever I went to Addis.

On one visit to her apartment, several of the Peace Corps were sitting around chatting and snapping fleas in half. No matter how classy a dwelling was in Ethiopia, the fleas were omnipresent. A roll of Scotch tape happened to be on a nearby table. I casually wrapped some tape around my hand and began to swat at the annoying pests. Soon I had collected dozens of fleas on it. They were thoroughly trapped! We all began to admire this new way to control fleas.

"Let's write a letter to the 3-M Company to let them know of this unique use for their product," I suggested. Ruth found an address and we used her typewriter to compose a letter. To demonstrate the usefulness of the tape, we dropped the portion of the tape, which was encrusted with dozens of fleas, into the envelope with the letter. We all laughed hysterically at our cleverness, and the picture that came into our heads when we imagined the look on the face of an official at the 3-M Company upon opening the letter.

A month later, Ruth alerted us to the arrival of a package from the 3-M Company. The letter attached to the package told us of their surprise at this most unusual use of their product. To make our stay in Ethiopia more pleasant, they had sent us a gross of Scotch tape! Creativity, and a little zaniness, can pay off!

CHAPTER 25
HALLOWEEN PARTY
AND A PROPOSAL

Our new contingent of Peace Corps Volunteers loved parties. They now were opening their homes for celebrations. Halloween was on the horizon. A costume party seemed to fit the bill. Everyone was talking about what kind of costume to make. We had to be creative with the few things available.

George had become a regular visitor at our house. I discovered his family called him "Bobby" with a delightful Southern drawl that he was great at imitating. His middle name was "Robert" so I began to call him "Bob." We shared a lot about our backgrounds. We had both been very active in our churches. Bob told of the time he had gone forward at a Billy Graham Crusade which had been held in a tent. He knew most of the hymns and gospel songs I liked. However, he was very silly and would periodically break into one of his hill-bill-y tunes, like, "My Uncle Bill has a Still on the Hill," or some other equally humorous ditty. We would laugh our heads off wondering if the tune would make the "Hit Parade" or if we would hear it on the BBC (British Broadcasting Network), the station which always came in clearly to Dessie. A new group out of Liverpool, England called "The Beatles" had a hit song "I Want to Hold Your Hand." Every time it was played on the BBC Bob grabbed my hand and jokingly said that that was our song.

For our Halloween costumes we decided to dress alike. The easiest costumes to make were those of pirates. I had several pair of black tights. We both had black pants that could be rolled up. Green shirts would make our tops, and of course, a black patch over the eye would complete our get-ups. When we arrived at the party, there were over thirty people there. But no one else was in costume! We were the only two who looked ridiculous. Everyone else was normal—normal clothes, normal make-up, normal everything. Over and over again, our colleagues said, "You two were made for each other."

The evening was quite warm and the crowded rooms became a bit stifling. Bob suggested we take a walk in the balmy night air. A harvest moon was cresting over the mountain range behind our town. Hyenas could be heard hooting off in the distance. The other usual night sounds were all around us as we listened to the laughter and music from the party in a distance. A little bridge on the road crossed a bubbling stream beneath. We stopped and sat on the stones of the bridge looking out at the night sky. The world seemed somewhat hushed around us.

While looking off in a distance, Bob quietly said, "You know, I want you to be my wife."

I gasped, "Why in the world would you want that? I don't ever plan on marrying. My Mom and Dad had to struggle so hard to raise my 8 brothers and sisters and me. I want to travel, make an impact on the world, do something important. I've seen only difficulty in the marriages of my relatives. The last thing I want to do is bring children into the world."

"I don't care if we ever have children or not," said Bob. "I only want you to be a part of my life forever."

I was touched by his fervor and told him I was very flattered. My answer at this time was definite. "No, even if the others think we were made for each other," I said as I grinned at my "twin" in the pirate costume.

I was to learn over the next six months that this North Carolinian had extreme patience and would not take no for an answer.

A series of letters began to arrive daily at my door. They were filled with funny jokes, items from the news, Ethiopian trivia, gossip about our PCV crowd, school information, invitations to picnics with others and alone with Bob, flattering comments, and always closing with "I love you! XXX-YYY-XXX." The stack of letters grew by the week. For some reason I kept them.

Bob's messenger was one of his students who lived at his compound. The boy's name was Belayneh Gebre. Some of Bob's letters told the background of this student. Belay had been born in the village of Meskala at 16,000 feet, high above Dessie. As a child he had herded sheep and cattle. When rows of sorghum, teff and other grains were planted in his father's fields, he and his friends sat up in towers of woven branches with slingshots to scare off the birds. His family had wanted him to be a Coptic priest and had sent him to the little village church school to learn to read and write Amharic, to understand numbers, and to learn to chant. Belay did not like to sing and chant. He loved learning all the other material and was an outstanding student. He did not want to become a priest.

People traveling through Meskala on their way to market started to tell the villagers how the Emperor had invited many teachers to come to Ethiopia. A group of teachers, called the Peace Corps from America, were to begin teaching in Dessie at Woizero Siheen Secondary School. This government school was a six day journey down steep mountain trails, only wide enough for donkeys, goats, sheep, a horse or two, or people walking two abreast. There was one mountain range after another between Meskala and Dessie.

Belay began to ask numerous questions of the travelers from below. Where did they get water to drink along the way? Where did they stop at night? Were there many hyenas or jackals? Did they go through many small villages? Were people kind? Plans began to take shape. Belay finally had the courage to tell his family that he wanted to be taught by the Peace Corps teachers who were coming to Dessie. His father was very upset. His mother cried. But he was determined.

He was fourteen when he began his journey across the mountain

157

ranges to go to school in Dessie. He wore shorts and had a "gobby" slung over his shoulders. A "gobby" was a tightly woven cotton blanket that was very warm. It could even be piled on the head to protect one from sunshine. He also had a small woven basket for "injerra," bread to be eaten along the way. Belay had never worn shoes. The bottoms of his feet were thick and sturdy. He also carried a "jib stick" or pole for shaking at hyenas and for steadying himself on the steep trails. The pole was also useful for catching fish in fresh water streams that trickled and flowed down the mountainside.

One early morning Belay decided to begin his journey, following the mountain trail that went down and down and then wove up for awhile. In places the pathway went around the sides of mountains that had steep drop-offs. Then meadows would appear. As dusk arrived, Belay looked for a "sar bet." At each hut he asked if he could curl up and sleep outside. Even the poorest Ethiopian was happy to have a visitor, and he was always invited to sleep inside and to partake of the meager meal. Wrapped in his "gobby" and with some nourishment inside his stomach, he slept well. Some dwellers even sent him forth the next day with pieces of injerra to fill his empty basket. Others had further directions for his journey. Cool mountain streams kept him refreshed. Each day he clambered down further and further with some ranges that had to be climbed up and then down again. He was now far from Meskala.

After six days of walking, Belay arrived in Dessie. The first motorized vehicles he saw scared him. They passed him so rapidly on the street that they were gone before he could believe what he had seen. Thank goodness that they were noisy so he could prepare himself for them. The streets were bustling with rumbling motor trucks and cars, horse-drawn gherrys, boys herding sheep and goats, and men and women carrying loads on their backs or heads. It was exciting to be in such a big city. Many streets even had a smooth black topping on them. It was neater than the dusty, dirt roads in Meskala and the gravel and dirt trails he had just traversed for six days.

He asked directions to Woizero Siheen School. Already dozens of boys like him were standing around or sitting on the ground waiting to register for school. Most were quite excited saying that they had seen some of the American teachers walking around the school compound. As dusk came to Dessie, Belay was amazed at the lights that came on in the storefronts facing the piazza. Some of the boys explained that Dessie even had electricity! Black top roads, motor vehicles and electricity! This certainly was NOT Meskala!

One of the boys said that he heard the Peace Corps was going to set up a lunch program of injerra and wat. Many of the students were used to only one meal a day. With that meal, their gobbies to roll up in, they could sleep against some wall. During daylight they could study. With a little begging now and then for paper and a pencil, they were, indeed, ready for their education.

After several days of sleeping near the school fence, one of the boys told Belay that he had heard that some of the Peace Corps were taking in students who had come from far away. Belay, who had Bob and Marc for teachers, made inquiries. He became one of the lucky ones to live on the Peace Corps compound.

All this information about the boy who delivered Bob's letters to me was written over a period of time. I was not sure which male intrigued me the most. It was obvious that Bob enjoyed getting to know his Ethiopian students too. This endeared him to me in a new way. The details Bob wrote about Belay indicated how special Belay had become to him. I admired that in him. It showed compassion. I would like that in a husband.

But marriage? Now? Not possible!

CHAPTER 26
VISITS FROM DIGNITARIES:
SHRIVER, WOFFORD,
ROCKWELL AND OTHERS

It was November of our first year in Ethiopia. The school compound was abuzz with excitement. Our head master appeared to be somewhat flustered. The Ethiopian and Indian teachers were excitedly talking among themselves. We kept hearing the name, Kennedy, in the midst of their rapid conversations. Finally the Peace Corps teachers were called together and told that just that morning, a call had been received from Addis Abeba. Sargent Shriver, who had been appointed to head President Kennedy's newly formed Peace Corps, had arrived in Ethiopia and wished to see one of the towns where the Peace Corps was working.

Ethiopians hold family ties in high regard, no matter how distant the relationship. Shriver and Kennedy were cousins. President Kennedy's mother, Rose Kennedy was the sister of Shriver's mother. Having Sargent Shriver in our village was like a visit from royalty!

In addition, Harris Wofford, the Head of the Peace Corps in Africa, was also on the same plane, which was to arrive shortly. Wofford was a former Senator from Pennsylvania before his appointment by Kennedy.

Both Shriver and Wofford wanted to meet with us. Shriver thanked all of the volunteers for being among the first Peace Corps groups. He stated that the President wanted all of us to have a positive and healthy experience. The importance of the Peace Corps' impact on Third World countries was stressed. He reminded us that we were also in Ethiopia by the invitation of the Emperor who wanted to bring his country into the modern era. These two important men circulated and talked with us and with our headmaster. They were at our school for a short two hour period and had to be off to other locations in the country. Our Dessie group of volunteers felt quite honored by this visit.

In our second year we had a visit of a very different kind. We knew ahead of time that the famous American painter and artist for the *Saturday Evening Post*, Norman Rockwell, was going to be staying in our town for several days. He was coming here to find ideas for a picture about the Peace Corps in Ethiopia. He wanted an example of volunteers in the field for one of the up-coming issues of the magazine. He wanted his illustration to be representative of the work done by Kennedy's new program, as young Americans worked with people in a Third World country. Rockwell and his wife stayed at the home of the four male PCV's across the street from us. Marc and Bob had given their room over to these guests.

Rockwell, a tall and slender grey-haired gentleman, and his wife, a petite grey-haired lady, asked many questions about the daily tasks of the volunteers in Dessie. They visited a number of us to see what we did and took numerous photos. Since their visit was on a weekend and school was not in session, the pictures had to be posed. Mrs. Rockwell, who was in charge of the photography equipment for her husband, helped to pose individuals as Mr. Rockwell watched and coached. Then a series of photos were taken. One photo set was with a Peace Corps nurse who sat and held a baby on her lap in front of a mud hut. The one that became the main subject of Rockwell's choice was Marc Clausen posing with some farmers in a field explaining the use of a plow. Mrs. Rockwell was very exacting that some of the mountains be in the background. The plow had to be repositioned several times. Then she showed how she wanted the subjects to place their arms and lean in as if listening to each other. Numerous photos were taken again. Rockwell used the photos that were taken to assist him with his paintings when he returned home.

When the Rockwell's left, we had no idea whether he would be selecting a choice from Ethiopia or some other country. We were all delighted to see the picture of Marc and the Ethiopians with the plow in the centerfold of one of the issues of *The Saturday Evening Post.* But more recently, a series of U.S. postal stamps came out to "Celebrate the Century." A set of the stamps highlighted events of the 60's. One of the stamps was the one Norman Rockwell had done of the Peace Corps in Ethiopia.

Over the years we had stayed in touch with Marc, who had been best man at our wedding in Ethiopia and Rome. He stated that many friends who saw the stamp believed him to be dead. Most stamps only depict people who are deceased. However, this stamp was depicting the Peace Corps in general, not the people on the stamp. We were sure Marc's friends were relieved to discover that he was still alive and well. Even forty plus years later we have remained in contact with Marc and we visit each other.

Other personages of distinction visited our town, but many of them were lesser know to the world. We grew to love a woman named Pearl Campbell who stayed at my home several times. She worked with U.S.I.S. libraries and facilitated the setting up of a library at Woizero Siheen School. Her husband had some important position in the U.S. Embassy in Addis. Pearl was always giving motherly advice to all of the single Peace Corps women. She and her husband had traveled all over the world. "To keep your man," she would say, "always have flowers on your table and eat by candlelight, even if you're only serving hot dogs or peanut butter and jelly sandwiches." I've tried to remember this over the years. Later, my husband and I used to even put a lit candle in a holder on the floor by our pets' dishes of food. I guess Pearl left an impact on me.

U.S. Postal Service Peace Corps Stamp

In 1998 the U.S. Postal Service selected, with a vote of the public, fifteen events symbolizing the 1960's. Images honoring the Walk on the Moon, Martin Luther King's "I Have a Dream" speech, the Beatles, the Vietnam War, the Peace Corps, and various other happenings which became a series of stamps entitled "Celebrate the Century."

On the Peace Corps stamp was a Volunteer working with a group of Ethiopian farmers. The image was a replica of a painting by Norman Rockwell, the well-known American artist. This particular painting had first appeared in the center of the *Saturday Evening Post* in the sixties.

Norman Rockwell and his wife stayed at the Dessie home of four Peace Corps Volunteers. Rockwell's wife was very exacting in positioning the group in the photo to pose. Dozens of placements of individuals in the group were done with great detail given to the background. Camera shots accompanied each new position. It was years later when we saw the final results.

The Volunteer in the photo is Marc Clausen, Bob's roommate for the two years in Dessie and Best-man at our wedding ceremonies in Addis and later in Rome, Italy.

CHAPTER 27
THE ASSASSINATION OF
PRESIDENT KENNEDY

The evening of November 22, 1963 had begun so pleasantly. Carol, Bob and I had been visiting the homes of some of the new PCV's. We finished the evening by stopping at the fellows' house across the street. As we were sitting around chatting, the door flew open and Arwilda, who was always calm, poised, immaculate in appearance, and always in control, came flying through the door. She was in her housecoat and slippers, hair in curlers and extremely upset. Her trembling voice shouted, "Kennedy has been shot! I just heard it on 'Voice of America'!"

We all dashed across the street to our house, shouting as we ran, "This can't be true." "There must be some mistake." "Maybe there was some slight accident." We kept repeating other inane phrases as we tried to reassure each other. The radio was on as we entered the house and pushed ourselves to the doorway of Arwilda's room. Now the announcer was saying that the President was dead! We were instantly shocked to stunned silence! Then we all began to weep and fall into each other's arms for consolation.

We listened through our quiet sobs and tears about the terrible events of the day in Dallas. The President's entourage had driven from the airport through the streets of the city. The whole distance was packed with throngs of cheering people, three and four deep, lining the sides of the roads and waving at the open convertible where this much loved and admired President sat with his beautiful wife. Jack and Jackie, as they were lovingly called by millions, had smiled and waved back to their adoring crowds.

Suddenly, as the car caravan neared a park, loud repercussions sounded from high up in a building. Heads turned, thinking someone had set off some fire crackers. No one could believe that rifle shoots had been fired. The crowd saw the President slump over into Jackie Kennedy's lap as she bent over and cradled his head. We heard how the Secret Service men jumped onto the President's vehicle to cover his body and how the car raced off to the hospital. Another official was also seriously injured. At the hospital, JFK was declared dead.

The announcer continued on but we were all too distraught to listen any further. This handsome young President, who had filled us with such hope and was so loved by much of the world, was now taken away from us by some stupid assassin's terrible act! We collapsed into chairs and wept throughout the night. It all seemed so incredulous! Had this really happened? Was it only a nightmare? Would we wake up to a bright new morning filled with sunshine?

Just last week we had witnessed two men who had been hung in our market place in town. Everyone had been talking about this. The culprits had been two young men who had killed their father, so the story went. The rapid judgment and punishment of those two men, had left me feeling as if I had been suddenly zapped into an old Western town in America of a 100 years ago.

All of this paled as dawn broke. Arwilda, who was from a little town near Dallas, was so upset that our President had been shot in Dallas. It was difficult to comprehend what had happened in such a few hours. We had continued to listen to "Voice of America" much of the night. They kept broadcasting about the President's assassination. Had this all just happened yesterday? Cells phones did not exist at this time. We all wondered how this was impacting the lives of our families back home. This tragic event in history hung over all of us. How would this affect the Civil Rights Movement? Or Foreign policy? What were world leaders thinking right now? What will

Kruschev's next moves be? What might Cuba do? We had followed the Bay of Pigs standoff in *Newsweek* and *Time* magazines. We could only imagine the enormity of the task placed on Vice President Lyndon Johnson at this moment. As we made coffee to wake us up after a sleepless night, we heard the murmuring of voices and shuffling of feet outside our door. Sound of weeping and wailing were coming from our yard. We looked out to see a mass of villagers sitting on the ground while others stood, heads uncovered, tears streaming down the faces of everyone. Some stood out in the road and others leaned against the fence posts and trees. Many were dressed in brown sack cloth. Some had scratched their face and thrown ashes over their heads and clothing. They had heard over the BBC in the piazza of President Kennedy's assassination. Little did the world know to what extent this American President was loved, admired and respected, even in remote towns like Dessie. As we stood in our doorway weeping, many of the mourners raised their hands to the heavens and loudly wailed, calling out to God. We moved among the crowd. They grasped our hands and bowed their heads. Over and over again I heard people say, "Eg'sahv'yer y'marsh, Eg'sahv'yer United States." "God bless you, God bless the United States." We all openly wept together

Throughout the day, townspeople, teachers, our head-master, and students stopped at the Peace Corps homes expressing their sympathy about the President. They wept with us and stated their deep concern for our welfare. Since Kennedy had begun the Peace Corps, would we be thrown into prison if we return to the United States? Would there be a revolution and much blood shed? What was going to happen in America now? They were truly worried for us. Several city officials said that we could make our homes forever in Ethiopia, become citizens here and not have to worry about returning home. Many believed that we would be in grave danger. They also wondered if we would all be called back to the U.S. immediately.

In the midst of our sorrow, the sincere concern of our many

167

Ethiopian acquaintances touched us deeply and brought some smiles back to our faces. We explained that the Constitution of the United States of American contained laws for succession in any eventuality. Our Vice President would be sworn is as the new president. They found it difficult to understand how this would come about so quickly and smoothly, without bickering, quarreling, and insurrections among officials. I don't think they believed us the first few days after the tragedy. Later they heard over the BBC, that Vice President Lyndon B. Johnson had been sworn in as President 38 minutes after Kennedy was declared dead. This was when a number of the teachers expressed amazement at American Democracy. Despite this horrible, wasteful murder of JFK, I am so thankful to come from our constitutional democracy where law is upheld.

Our 19 year old houseboy, Kamaal,, noticed how sad and depressed Arwilda, Carol and I were about the assassination. He made us a banana cake. It was frosted with white icing, and with food coloring. He had decorated the top of the cake with a vase and flowers. Above the flowers he wrote, "Enjoy it." How thoughtful!

The flag in our piazza flew at half-mast for forty days after the President's death. Ethiopia went into mourning. Many people wore completely black or completely white clothing for many weeks out of respect for the assassinated American president. How amazing it was that this country on the opposite side of the world with less than ten per cent literacy had been so filled with admiration for JFK. For many months after Kennedy was killed, villagers continued to express their condolences to us. We were touched by their sincere expressions of grief.

CHAPTER 28
WINTER PROBLEMS AND HOLIDAYS

Cold rain had been pelting down much of the time since JFK's assassination. The whole town looked as if it had been swallowed in a cloud. The cold winter rains had returned. Students, wrapped in blanket-like white gobbeys, were not complaining about sitting three to a desk. They huddled together now to share warmth. Only body heat warmed the room. I had been wearing a wool skirt and sweater, black tights, and my warm black coat. The cloud cover over the mountains and the mist in the valley gave a semblance of winter with snow about to appear. Only the green trees, bushes and grass near the classroom window could be seen through the wet mist. It still wasn't as bad as a Wisconsin winter. I've had to move some of the desks around in the room. A leak in the roof was the reason. A number of students were absent today because the mountain paths turn muddy and slippery in this weather. The mud became slicker than ice when these heavy rains commenced. The rocks in the road became extremely slick! Falling down in an ocean of mud is not as clean as sliding down on ice!

The rain fell quite interestingly here. There was almost no wind. The water seemed to fall from the heavens in straight streams all parallel to each other. When the clouds and fog lifted, the plants and leaves looked freshly washed as the rain carried the dust away.

All life seemed to stop during the rain. All the people, who just a few minutes before the rain, were bustling around the markets and shops, pasturing their animals, or washing in the river, had all disappeared. Even the animals were nowhere to be seen.

This period of the year was referred to as the "little rains." They usually lasted only a few weeks. However, this was also the coldest time of the year here. We could see our breath in the chilly morning and night air. This weather made it difficult to believe that I was in Africa! The other day we had big, white balls of hail that fell from the sky. The students were excited about it and called it snow. They even made balls of hail to throw at one another!

The rain poured so hard on the tin roof of the classroom that it was difficult to hear or be heard. My classes had been writing themes on what they thought about when it rained. Many still talked about President Kennedy's assassination and wrote that the heavens were still mourning his tragic death. They wrote how their family and friends were terribly shaken by this event. They never thought something like that could have happened in America.

The sun still managed to poke its shining warmth through the clouds for a brief period each day during this season. It actually stayed sunny but cool during our Thanksgiving celebration, which was a bit more subdued this year. All the PCV's celebrated together with turkey, stuffing and all the trimmings.

We had an interesting learning experience about justice and the law here in Dessie. Someone had climbed through our storage room window which is high off the ground and, thus, the only window left unlocked in our house. Footprints on the outside wall under the window, gave us the clue. The store room was where we kept our water filter, ironing board and clothing to be ironed. The thief stole clothing, bedding, a rug, and an umbrella. Then the thief attacked a week later. We had put two students on watch for us. However, they fell asleep on chairs in our front room. The thief was startled by their movements and quickly ran away with nothing. We went to the police and reported the crimes. The house was locked up and well secured.

The first sunny day we had, prompted us to have a big wash hung out on our clothes lines. People here, apparently had not seen clothes lines before. Most spread the newly washed items on the ground to dry. That, of course, left the laundry rather dusty on one side. Villagers found our drying technique intriguing and we began to see more and more clothes lines going up.

On this particular wash day, we had been eating lunch at the table in our house watching the clothing blowing gently in an afternoon breeze. Suddenly we saw a brown arm reaching up and removing items from the line. It was not our houseboy, Kamaal, since he was in the room with us. We went running outside as the thief went running down the street with a pile of our laundry in his arms. We chased after him hollering, "Layba! Layba!" "Thief! Thief!" Several boys, who were herding goats down the road, tackled the middle-aged man and hauled him off to the prison in town. We were able to retrieve our laundry which was scattered all over the road.

A few days later, a magistrate appeared at our door requesting our appearance in court for the man's trial. We said we did not wish to press any charges since our belongings had been retrieved. The official said that "it was the custom of the country to try the wrong-doer." We were given a day and time to report to the prison where the trial was to be held.

Upon arrival in the courtroom at the prison, Carol, Arwilda and I were given wooden chairs on which to sit. Everyone else was standing except the judge and the three of us since soldiers were ordered to bring chairs for us. The thief was brought forward. We didn't understand everything that was going on, but there was plenty of pointing at us and at the thief. We weren't certain if it was for our benefit or for teaching a lesson to the culprit, but sentence was quickly passed.

Several soldiers held the sentenced thief under his armpits and led him outside. We were told to follow. The thief was led to a bench and his arm was stretched out on top of a wooden plank. Within seconds a vicious looking curved sword appeared and before anyone knew what was happening, the man's arm was chopped off as he screamed and collapsed! Another soldier took a torch and held the burning flame to the gaping, bleeding wound to cauterize it. Standing near this horrifying scene were several little children with a woman. They appeared to be the brutalized man's family. They wept and wailed. We stood stunned and shocked. We barely heard the magistrate when he came up to us. "Our laws are Biblical and they are swift. He will steal no more." Several soldiers were dispatched to carry the man home.

Dazed and horrified we slowly returned to our home. We would have gladly let that man keep our laundry if we had known the outcome! What could we do now? We had some of our students make inquiries about the family. Quietly, since we felt guilty and ashamed, we bundled up bedding, towels, and clothing. We pooled together some money and food and sent it to the man and his family. We sent food and money to the family during the rest of our stay here. This horrifying punishment taught us a part of Ethiopia we did not like. It left us quite subdued and gave us a lot to ponder.

The rains began to subside as we neared Christmas. The weather remained cool. We put up a little tree and strung the Christmas cards we had all received last year, in the windows. Some teachers at Peckham had sent a little sparkling tree and a Santa Claus, which I put up. We brought in a few sprigs of cedar to add a holiday scent to the house. It was looking Christmas-y! The tree was decorated with home-made decorations again. We miss lights for the tree. I don't think the guys across the street will experiment with candles this year after their fiasco last Christmas!

Twenty-five of us PCV's went out to the Leprosarium for Christmas Eve. It was a pleasant get-together. We played games, sang carols, saw a filmstrip on the Christmas story, and ate all kinds of goodies. The night was very foggy and cold. As we drove out to the SIM compound, the fog was so thick that we felt as if we were driving through a blizzard back in Wisconsin. It rained so we could do no caroling outside for the lepers this year.

On Christmas Day in the morning, eight of us gave a choir concert of a sort for the Lutheran Mission in town. There were 2 sopranos, 2 altos, 2 tenors, and 2 bases. Ron Bell directed us and Liz played the pump organ. We enjoyed singing and our listeners seemed to enjoy it too. Afterward we were invited for cookies and coffee by the missionaries. In the afternoon my household exchanged presents and opened gifts we got from the States.

The weather started to change for the better and Bob took me on a picnic to another mountain range called "Doro Meslaya." We shared a lot about our families. He wanted to get a Masters Degree at Columbia University in New York City. I was not too sure what I wanted to do after the Peace Corps other than to return to Milwaukee to teach. Several of our close friends, Marc, Gene, and Don were planning on remaining for a third year. Bob had driven one of the jeeps to the trail head where our hike had begun. He carried the picnic lunch. At the top of the mountain we had a view of Dessie from a totally different direction. Dozens of little children followed behind us. We were a little distance from town, so these young ones hadn't seen the "ferengis" very much. We were now used to the giggling and covering of faces whenever we spoke to anyone for the first time. It was dark by the time we arrived back in Dessie. Bob had come prepared with some lamb and chicken bones. We drove to one of the open meadows, threw the bones out of the window, drove about 20 feet away, turned off the head lamps, and waited. Within 10 minutes we heard some passing noise. Suddenly the silence was broken by loud whooping sounds. Bob switched on the head lights and there they were—three hyenas munching away on the bones! "Shining hyenas" turned this time into a very unusual date! Bob was still asking me to marry him. My reply was still no. But it was nice that he kept asking.

School examinations began on December 30th. School closed on January 6th. In between correcting exams, we worked on the grand opening of the USIS [United States Information Service] library. It was located downstairs in the newer wing of our school. We worked day and night getting it in order. Some of us worked on drapes for the windows, others helped type the cards for the books. We arranged books on the shelves and placed the furniture and flowers around the room. The library was looking very modern and inviting. There were even some stuffed chairs for reading comfortably. Pearl Campbell used the other twin bed in my room while she supervised our activities at the school. A number of officials from Wollo Province attended the grand opening. Most in attendance had never seen anything quite like our new library. They were eager to check out books. Some were happy just to sit in a stuffed chair.

New Year's Eve was pretty uneventful. Bob came over and we corrected exams. The other PCV's still called him "George," but since he shared how his family had always called him "Bobby" from his middle name "Robert," I have been calling him "Bob." I kept learning more about him. He graduated from Guillford College, a Quaker school in North Carolina. A friend from childhood, Ruffin Pinckney Tucker, was also in the Peace Corps in India.

Bob wanted me to be part of the group of PCV's who were planning to go to Jerusalem. He continued to tell me that he loved me. Almost daily I was receiving love letters from Bob, which were faithfully delivered by his messenger, Belay. I reminded him that I enjoyed being with him, but I was, by no means, in love.

We had each received some money from the Peace Corps and, with the money I received as gifts from home at Christmas, I was now able to join the group of about 83 PCV's going to Jerusalem. I really appreciated the Christmas dollars I received. A bunch of us drove to Addis to get some travelers' checks. Bob went to the evening service at the SIM with me. I had been asked to sing for services several times. This time I sang "The Love of God" and "How Great Thou Art." Prior to the service we were invited to dinner. The missionaries at SIM headquarters knew how much PCV's loved having a genuine American dinner.

Addis had become such a modern city since we arrived. New

buildings were sprouting up everywhere. New roads were being built. Florescent street lamps light the boulevards at night. The University was growing. An art center, where concerts were performed, had been built. So much was happening in this capital city. I wondered what it would look like in ten years.

The next day we drove back to Dessie, and hurriedly packed for our drive north to Asmara where we caught our plane to Jerusalem. After settling into an old convent where once again I was the roommate of Carol Wood, we had a full day scheduled.

At our gathering place outside the convent, we were surprised that a bus wasn't taking us around. Instead we were led to beautiful 1962-63 Dodges to begin our sight-seeing. We soon learned that buses would not have been practical nor safe through all the narrow, winding streets. Our car sped through the alley-like streets, allowing only a couple of inches between cars and buildings. We drove out the Dung Gate on the road to Bethany to see Lazarus' Tomb and the home of Mary and Martha. Next we drove to the Dead Sea where we saw the ruins of the Essenes and the caves where the Dead Sea Scrolls were found. From here we went to the Jordan River to see the place where John had baptised Christ. Then we drove to Jericho but it was getting too dark to see much.

The cars brought us back to our hotel for dinner. After eating, we explored the bazaars on our own. Bazaars, which line all the narrow streets, sold all kinds of jewelry, brass and brocades. I didn't buy anything the first night.

The next day we were up early and drove to Bethlehem. On the way we stopped at Rachel's tomb. We finally reached the Church of the Nativity. All of the major places devoted to the life of Christ were taken over by Catholics, Armenians or Greek Orthodox groups. There was even an Ethiopian Coptic Church in the middle of a tangle of small streets. The original sites are canopied by huge cathedrals, and the "actual spots" were dripping with draperies, chandeliers, incense burners, or other paraphernalia. It seemed a little over-the-top to me.

175

In the afternoon we were back in Jerusalem and visited the Holy Sepulcher and where Calvary was supposed to have been. Somehow I found it difficult to accept that Calvary was inside this gigantic church. We walked through the market place to where Mary had been born, and then to the Pool of Bethesda where Jesus healed the man who had been lame for 38 years.

After dinner we returned to the bazaars and sampled different kinds of Jordanian candies.

On the third day we visited the Mount of Olives. From here we could see all of Jerusalem, even over into Israel. We went to the Garden of Gethsemane and several other churches. In the afternoon we followed the way of the cross which Christ took on his way to Calvary.

Saturday, instead of following the regular schedule, five of us rented a car and took the five hour drive to Damascus in Syria. On the way we could see the snow-capped mountains of Lebanon. We had to get visas before crossing the border. On the way our car was stopped 11-15 times by police. They checked our visas and passports. The same thing happened on our return. It reminded us of what police states these countries are. We were glad to be Americans.

Damascus is one of the oldest cities in the world. But it was also modern. We came mainly to visit the old covered market place. I was amazed by the remains of beautiful Roman arches and columns all around us in this ancient market place. The stalls of the bazaars were built right around the bases of these ancient structures. People seemed to be carrying on their business completely oblivious to all the history those arches and columns signified. Here I bought all kinds of things, from Muslim prayer rugs, to Damask table cloths, to Turkish coffee sets. We were here only a few hours and then had to return to Jerusalem.

Sunday morning Carol and I rose early to go to see the Dome of the Rock. This is the place where King Solomon had built his temple. Way before him, Abraham had been sent by God to sacrifice his son,

Isaac on this spot. The Muslims claim Mohammed ascended to heaven from this spot. A beautiful, huge mosque with a golden dome now covers the area, thus, "The Dome of the Rock." It is now called the Mosque of Omar. We were allowed inside the mosque where we were able to see the original rock.

I was impressed to see everyone busy and working wherever we went in Jordan. We saw no one in rags or dirty clothes—and we saw no beggars. When we arrived back in Ethiopia, we were reminded of how much this country was still underdeveloped. This five day trip was kind of an eye-opener to us. So much was seen and done in that short time. Bob had arranged to be with me on all the tours. I think he enjoyed the number of adventures in the evenings when we visited market places and bargained for treasures. I am a very good bargainer. After each price was finally agreed upon, the shop keeper would call for hot Turkish coffee to be served to clinch the deal.

What a full Holiday period this was. Our last semester here in Ethiopia was soon to begin.

CHAPTER 29
PROBLEMS, JOY AND SADNESS

The cold rain and fog had finally subsided and the sun shone early in the morning now. It was interesting how, even during the month of foggy cold weather, the sun still came out for an hour or two at midday. This country was aptly named, "The Land of 13 Months of Sunshine." With sun now shining gloriously, the mountains, foliage, homes, fields and everything looked freshly washed and stunningly beautiful.

There had been a few problems at the school. Our first head-master, Ato Yifru Gebayahu, was transferred to the new school built by the Russians in Bahar Dar during our second year. We were somewhat pleased at first to see him go. He was not very pro-Peace Corps ever since we arrived, even though the PCV's were the only teachers who reported to class regularly. Many of the other instructors did not report to school whenever the head-master was gone, which was quite frequently.

We went through a series of replacements. The first new head-master who arrived, was a Muslim and of a different tribal background from the majority of the students. Most of the students were Coptic Christians and from the Amhara tribe. A growing restlessness resulted at the school. Two serious fights broke out among the students of different tribes. A discipline committee was formed to try to handle the situations. A number of suspensions were made, and it seemed to quiet down the restlessness and resentment somewhat. We all hoped the situation would improve.

My own English classes continued to be an absolute delight. The students were so excited about their own progress with the use of

English, which, of course, made me feel quite proud. I will miss my students tremendously when I leave.

Problems continued to plague us at school. Our new head-master was not forceful enough for our students. Many of the teachers, including a few PCV's were finding students becoming rowdy. Problems had arisen among some of the girls in the Girls' Club. One of the girls in my homeroom was accused of being a harlot and was being dismissed from the school. She had come to me in tears and sobbing that she was innocent. The head-master said there was much evidence against her, but I was never told what it was. I offered to take her to a Peace Corps woman doctor to verify claims of her virginity, but was told that that was "against the custom" here. It was extremely frustrating to me and I felt terrible for the girl.

Demonstrations had broken out against Somalia. Everyone in our town had heard of the fighting on the Ethiopia/Somali borders, which overlapped the Ogaden Desert. This desert, in the eastern and northeastern portion of Ethiopia, spanned the borders of both countries. Most news of the fighting came over the radio broadcasts in the piazza. The fighting was sounding pretty severe. The quarrel was over border disputes between the two countries. Somali nomadic tribes regularly herd their cattle and camels across the desert in this region. They had a tendency to periodically settle on the part of the Ogaden Desert which was in Ethiopia. Since so many had wandered across into Ethiopia, they felt they had "squatters' rights to the territory. In addition, they reminded everyone that the borders, like so many in Africa, were determined by the British years ago. Unfortunately, this argument needed another court for settling claims on boundary disputes throughout Africa. Disputes like this would continue to arise until the Organization of African States and the United Nations formed some kind of a policy on the many border problems throughout Africa.

Since the students were so upset about the news, they decided to demonstrate against Somalia. Peace Corps rules stated that we couldn't take part in political activities, so we had to stand by and observe. The students made large placards and posters and attached them to poles to be carried around. The band played and the students marched from the school to the Governor's office, singing songs in praise of Ethiopia and against Somalia. The demonstration was quite jovial. One would never have thought this to be about war. Only the placards carried strong language. This all appeared to be a way for students to get an extra day off from school.

People at home didn't have to worry about us. We were so hemmed in by high mountains, that it would make warfare here almost impossible. Also, we were far away from any battles. I couldn't feel safer!

We had several days off for some more national holidays. I went to Mai Chow, a village about 300 kilometers north of Dessie, to visit with Kay MacLeod, another SIM nurse. She was only a few years older than me. The visit was unique since Mai Chow is a very tiny village with no electricity or plumbing. All of the water came from a pump outside the house. There was one other couple on this station. Kay had to run the clinic while I visited. I became her temporary housekeeper and cook, making the meals for us—stuffed cabbage, spaghetti, and curried chicken. I went with Kay on one of her visits to a tukul in the village. The man living there was ill. He had had a curse placed on him three months ago. Now, he was suffering headaches from it. Although Kay gave him medicine, it is difficult to handle or fight curses. Many nationals have deep beliefs in the power of curses and the work of witch doctors. My visit at Mai Chow had been very enlightening.

Upon returning to Dessie I discovered that we were again without a head-master at our school. The third headmaster was in a serious car accident coming up our mountain. Students were becoming even more rowdy. Many of the Ethiopian and Indian teachers had not been going to their classes. As a result their students were causing such a commotion on the school compound, that those teachers, who were in their classrooms, were finding it difficult to teach. Something had to be done to stop the situation from getting out of hand. This situation went on for over a week. We went through three more replacements. None of them was able to maintain discipline. They all wanted to be liked by the students and faculty. They were afraid to give orders and did not know how to be firm. The main Ethiopian in charge of the school now was an Ethiopian Counselor/Vice Principal. He was feared and hated by the students because he carried a switch and never hesitated to mete out corporal punishment. Many of the teachers preferred this form of discipline. Most of the PCV's were beginning to feel a bit relieved that we had only four more months to go. It was difficult to endure such man-handling of students. I hated to leave here with bad impressions when I had really enjoyed these two years.

We had a wedding reception recently for one of our newly married Peace Corps couples here in Dessie. Two more couples were getting married in July. It seemed as if a "bug" had taken over.

Last Sunday evening Bob took me to dinner at the Italian Touring Hotel in town. He talked about taking his Master's Degree at Columbia University in New York City, North Carolina University, or the University of Northern Illinois. He had make applications to all and was eager to see which would provide the best financial help for him. Travel plans home were discussed. I told him that I had been planning to travel across Europe with Arwilda and Cindy Tse. He made no more proposals to me. We discussed the importance for him to receive his Master's degree.

I guess I kind of like this silly guy.

Lakech and Kebede came over for one of their frequent visits. They brought me a big papaya. This young couple was so dear to me. Lakech came by just last week to learn how to smock pillows. She learns how to do everything so rapidly. Her baby was due in another month, just about exam time. She said she planned to go to school until the very end. I was afraid the baby would be born at school! Lakech was in a classroom next to my room. I may have to assist in the

181

delivery! Perhaps another "first" was to come before I leave here. Kebede was working on permission for Lakech to have her exams given at home should the baby arrive at that time. I prayed our NEW head-master would be cooperative. I was really going to miss this young woman who had become such a good friend.

Lakech's baby was born today, March 24, 1964. She had a beautiful little girl. The baby was named Frehiwot, "Fruit of Life." I went to see the baby today as did many in town. Lakech was loved and respected by so many people. Kabede, Lakech and the baby were so happy. Each day at school, I inquired after the new family and heard only glowing reports of how well the mother and child were doing.

On Wednesday a week and a half after the baby's birth, several girls who had been close friends of Lakech last year, came to my house at lunch. I was struck by their serious demeanor as they asked me if I had Aspirin or any sleeping pills. When I made inquiries, they said Lakech was ill and couldn't sleep. She hadn't slept since Monday and was going "mad," repeating the same phrases over and over again, the girls said. I gave them a note for Kebede to take Lakech to the hospital right away. The girls looked doubtful and left with looks on their faces as if to say, "You don't really understand."

Being concerned, I left early for the afternoon school sessions, and stopped at Lakech's home first to see if things were under control. When I entered the yard, it was thronged with people. Upon entering the two room house, more people were packed to the walls. It was suffocating inside. I had to chase most of the people outside. When Lakech heard my voice, she cried out, "Miss Summers! Come! I am Mary, Lakech is dead! She will return in forty days." I went to her bedside where people were holding her convulsing body down. She continued a constant flow of incoherent jabber half in Amharic, half in English. She was Mary, Queen of Heaven, who had come to comfort Lakech, because no one else could. Lakech had always helped others, but there was no one to help her. Lakech had been so good; now she was dead. The pitiful gibberish flowed from her. When

I sat on her pallet, she threw her arms around me and said no one believed her. The priests had come and said that she was possessed by a devil. Then she threw herself out of bed and twirled around. I asked Kebede if I could send one of the girls for a doctor. Kebede, as everyone else present, did not think this "madness" could be treated medically. Such behavior was handled by priests with holy water and oftentimes, with being kept in chains.

One of the Peace Corps doctors arrived in a jeep and administered sedatives that calmed Lakech down. The doctor explained that this was usually a form of post-partum psychosis. Some cases can be cured overnight in a hospital, or they may take a long time to overcome, if ever. As Lakech was led out to our jeep to be taken to the hospital, the women tried to throw a cloth over her head. When they were unsuccessful, they wailed and spoke words I couldn't understand. Several of my young students explained to me that without a covering on Lakech's head, her evil spirit would now enter her daughter. Once again, I saw how superstition played an enormous role in the lives of these naïve people, educated or not.

Lakech was in the hospital from Wednesday to Saturday with no improvement. When I visited her, she babbled on as if out of her head. Her relatives removed her on Saturday to take her to a Coptic Church for the priests to pray, dance, chant, and throw holy water over her. It sounded like a form of exorcism. According to the relatives, after eight days of this, the evil spirit was supposed to come out. One of the Seventh Day Adventist doctors in town said that in a superstitious society such as this, such treatment may work more successfully than being in a hospital. Hospitals here weren't equipped to handle psychological patients for long periods or in severe cases.

Lakech's condition had become so depressing. Everyone at our school had expressed their dismay. I had never seen anything like this, and it was difficult to know what to make of it. Lakech was getting worse. Kebede took her to a village south of Addis where special holy waters for healing madness, were supposed to be located. So far, nothing had worked. Everything seemed so hopeless. It was terrible to think that Lakech could be "mad" the rest of her life. Some things were just too difficult to understand.

Lakech was taken to the Mental Hospital in Addis. She continued to be far from the brilliant young woman we all knew and loved. We all wondered if she would come out of her mental state. Things did not appear to be hopeful for her.

Spring exams had been given and corrected. Peace Corps termination meetings were to be held in Addis. I took the bus with Don Kilhefner to the capital. The bus made record time arriving in Addis by four in the afternoon. After getting checked in at the Peace Corps Hostel, we went to see a musical production of *Robin Hood* in Amharic put on by high school students. It was presented at the Haile Selassie University's Cultural Center. The talented singing, dancing and acting was enjoyed by everyone in attendance. Kids in the U.S. would have loved it, even if it was presented in this different language!

After a day of Peace Corps psychological tests to determine the impact of our experiences on us, we returned to our Hostel. Extremely sad news awaited me. Several PCV's who had just arrived from Dessie, told me that they had received distressing news concerning Lakech. Shock treatments had been given to Lakech at the Mental Hospital. Her weakened heart, which had become even more damaged over the past forty days, gave up. She had died two days ago May 5th. Her funeral was taking place today, May 7th in Dessie.

I was in a state of shock. I remembered seeing her at her home when she was babbling on and quite deranged. Her voice had said that Lakech would return in forty days. I was told by her friends that forty days had passed when Lakech had opened her eyes, asked about her child, and then closed her eyes in death. Her heart was too weak to say more. Everyone knew how much I had loved this brilliant and charming young girl who had wanted so much out of life. Part of me felt terrible that I hadn't been in Dessie for her funeral. Part of me felt relieved that the funeral had taken place before I returned.

After two more days of meetings in Addis, we returned to town by jeep. Dessie was still mourning for Lakech. All the girls at school and Lakech's friends from last year, were wearing black. I wore black. Some of the girls took me up to Lakech's grave site near St. Giorgis Church. We wept together as I placed flowers on the sad terrain. We spoke of the many accomplishments of our beloved friend, and shared favorite memories of her. Then we went to visit Kebede. He constantly wept and was eating nothing. Every time he looked at anything that had belonged to Lakech, he completely fell apart. He had lost much weight and appeared to be interested in nothing. There, in a cradle, slept the beautiful little child Lakech had left him to raise. A midwife sat nearby ready to attend to any need of the baby. Kebede had no parents and no one to whom he could turn. However, everyone in town had great respect for him. The students had asked me to also advise him. I had been trying to encourage him about his responsibility to his beautiful baby. He planned to raise the baby himself and had already hired several servants to help him. Frehiwot needed to be raised so that she would have all the education that Lakech had wanted. Kebede also needed to continue with his studies because this would have been pleasing to Lakech.

Since Lakech's death Kebede had not been allowed to be alone. All day long students filled the house and sat on the floor in silence. In the evening, all his friends and relatives gathered at his home. There seemed to be some psychology behind this. The evening visitors kept talking to Kebede and trying to keep him busy. After several weeks the mourning progressed to an interesting stage. Last night all the visitors were playing a game about an advocate who came to plead his case before a judge. There was much gaiety and laughter. The customs of this culture continue to amuse, entertain and, often, frustrate me.

Frehiwot was baptized 80 days after birth, as was the custom with girls. Boys were baptized 40 days after birth. Fre was a beautiful baby. I prayed she would have an easier life than her mother had and that she would fulfill the dreams of her mother.

CHAPTER 30
AN ENDING AND A BEGINNING

Our Dessie homes were looking bare. At the termination meetings in April, we were told that our sea freight to the U.S. would be picked up in the middle of May. The Ethiopian handiwork we had all been using for wall and table decorations had now been packed. Colorful woven baskets, plain basketry of all kinds, cups and birds made from animal horns, woven rugs, paintings of history and life in this country, carved wooden dolls, unusual metal jewelry and Coptic crosses, embroidery and clothing of the country, had all been secured in our trunks. I had also included lots of spices so the trucks should smell pleasantly fragrant! Oh, we even made another special trip to the Danikil Desert for the purchase of spears. We had to cut them in three parts to fit in our foot lockers. Most of my shoes, coats, sweaters and other clothing I have given to Ethiopian friends. The bedding, towels, pots, pans, dishes, and furnishings were to be left for the next group of PCV's. Only clothing for travel and some lovely Ethiopian gold and silver jewelry would be carried by me in my traveling luggage.

> *Dear Mom,*
> *I will miss our Dessie crowd! We have become good friends during the past two years. It will be so difficult to part. Most have not decided what they will do when they return home. I already mentioned that some were staying for a third year. I have not heard from the Milwaukee School Board*

A number of us plan to travel across Europe on our return. We can book all travel through the Peace Corps in Addis with our government paying the cost. Arwilda has already purchased a Eurail Pass for seeing as much of Europe as possible.

NOW FOR THE BIGGEST NEWS OF ALL! You are probably expecting this. Since Halloween Bob has been writing me numerous love letters and sending them by student messenger. Some were accompanied by flowers, others by candy. (I've always been a sucker for chocolate!) He begged me for the zillionith time to marry him. We know we don't want to part at the end of this Peace Corps experience. My resistance has broken down and I have accepted his proposal with the understanding that we receive your blessing.

You will soon be receiving a letter from Bob asking for your permission to marry me. You will notice that his full name is George Robert Parish. His entire family calls him, "Bobby" with a soft Southern accent. I think Bob has lost most of his Southern accent since coming to Ethiopia. He said his letter to you tells about his family. His dad works for an industry for the blind. He has two sisters and his mom has helped to raise many relatives.

Bob said that in his letter to you he wrote that marrying me was a great way to join together the North and the South—me being the Northerner from Wisconsin, and him being the Southerner from North Carolina.

I wrote to Bob's family as well, but I wasn't as clever.

Your Giddy Daughter

A few weeks later I received a precious response from my mom. She stated how happy she was for us and how wonderful Bob sounded in the letter. Her next comments tickled me. She asked if Bob was Black or White, since she remembered my former work with International Students at the University of Wisconsin-Milwaukee. Mom further stated that whatever he was, she knew I would make a perfect choice. She just wanted to prepare the family for our return!

Dear Mom,

I chuckled over your concern about Bob. He is very blond and blue-eyed which makes him look younger than his years. He is very thin. I will have to fatten him up. Maybe he will help me to shed some pounds! You know how I have always struggled with weight!

Bob can be really funny, with off-the-wall comments, which make people who first meet him question his intellectual abilities. However, his scholarships prove quite the contrast.

He comes from a very ordinary family too. It is an old Southern family with ancestors who fought in the Revolutionary and Civil Wars. He has traced his ancestry back to the French Huguenots who were Protestants. They escaped to Guildford County, England to prevent persecution from the Catholics in France. Centuries later his ancestors migrated to America and called their territory in North Carolina, "Guildford County."

Your Overly Joyous Daughter

In other letters home I told mom that Bob was from a Pilgrim Holiness background. However, Bob had been influenced by Quakers before and during his schooling at Guildford College, a Quaker institution. Some of his relatives had letters of manumission from assisting slaves to freedom on the Underground Railroad.

Bob told me that he had written his family about me four months ago when I was still fighting the thought of marriage. They had been telling him not to give up. They had already accepted me, even though I was a Yankee!

Bob was so happy with your letter to him. Did you receive a letter from his mom? Bob said she had written to you. He had just received a letter from his Mom saying that she was giving his dad English lessons. Dad's "Southernese" was so bad, according to her, and she wanted to impress me because I was an English teacher.

I told him that we lived in a highly integrated part of Milwaukee where Whites were in the minority. I also told him that our bathroom was in the basement. He laughed at that. Perhaps we had been trying to ease each other into our families.

Bob had received a scholarship from Columbia University in New York City and some government grant to cover expenses. He showed me a list of job openings in the area. I wrote to the Brooklyn New York Y.W.C.A. where a Program Director was needed. There were married student apartments on the campus of Columbia. The apartments were all two rooms with a kitchenette and bath, furnished. All we had to provide were cooking utensils, dishes, linens, curtains, table lamps, etc. I thought we would manage all right. We had learned to get along on so little in Ethiopia that we really didn't need much to get started. We were sure we would be able to get everything necessary in New York.

Dear Mom,
Thank you for the copy of the wedding
announcement you placed in the Milwaukee

Journal. *All plans seem to be moving along.*

Don't worry about wedding clothes. I bought material and a pattern. Arwilda is my Maid of Honor and she and I will make our dresses. The material we selected is a woven linen and our dresses will be lined in a nylon taffeta. Some of the other girls here have offered to help. There is a sewing machine at the Leprosarium and at the Seventh Day Adventist Mission, which is within walking distance. Smocking my head piece for my veil was Arwilda's suggestion. Our dresses will be very practical so we can wear them after the wedding for travel. They will have lace over-blouses to make them dressy for the wedding. Then I will make another jacket of matching material so I can use the outfit for travel. I will have to buy white shoes when we get to Rome. We will only have simple matching gold wedding bands because that is all we can afford. Ethiopian gold is 22 karat. It is very yellow and inexpensive here.

Our honeymoon will be our trip across Europe at Peace Corps expense.

Since we are being married out of the United States, we will need to have a civil ceremony in Ethiopia before we leave. The civil ceremony is a legal procedure that merely involves going to the American Embassy, having our names recorded in the census books, and signing a few documents. Bob is making arrangements for that. Marc and Arwilda will be the witnesses for me and the Mirkins will be the witnesses for Bob. This will take place on July 10th. The civil ceremony and the church ceremony can be in different countries.

On July 12th we fly to Rome, Italy where Bob has written letters to the Evangelical Mission. We will be married there on July 15th. Marc and Arwilda will accompany us and be Best Man and Maid of Honor at our wedding in this romantic city.

From Rome we will travel across Europe, take a plane from London to New York around August 10th. We will need to stay in New York a few days to get our confirmation on campus housing and registration for Bob. I will have a few job interviews. Then we will fly to Milwaukee. I can hardly wait to see everyone. We will be chewing each other's ears off! After Milwaukee we fly to Greensboro. We will be there in time to see Bob's sister graduate from nursing school. We must then return to NYC. School begins for Bob the second week of September.

Your Eager-to-see-you Daughter

Everyone here knew of our nuptials. The people at Boro Meda had a dinner for Bob and me. They invited the PCV's from our two houses. The dinner was an elegant one by candlelight. Afterwards, there were many funny games, much like at a shower. The lady missionaries had made matching travel kits for Bob and me. The kits had compartments for tooth brush, paste, soap, wash cloth and p. j.'s. They had made a pretty nightie for me and matching p.j.'s for Bob. They also presented us with a set of silver salt and pepper shakers that were hand-made and had the Lion of Judah on each. They were exquisite and small enough to fit easily in the corner of my suitcase.

Boro Meda had another engagement party the next week for *all* the couples who were getting married. Two other couples besides us had plans for getting married in July. One couple had been married the previous January. That gave our Dessie group the highest per cent of marriages for any city in which Peace Corps were stationed. At the party, we made wedding books from magazines and construction paper for all the couples. The books were hilarious. Of course there was the usual array of wonderful foods to eat. These missionaries had become my family. I wept inside to be leaving them. How greatly they would all be missed!

Every day we were invited for lunch and dinner to homes of various Ethiopian friends, and homes of the PCV II group, who would be remaining here. I was touched by the many who said, with great sorrow in their voices, that they would miss all of us. Only two weeks remained.

During our last week, the Girls' Club had a farewell party for me. They served a decorated cake and Fanta, an orange drink. They were happy about my up-coming marriage to "Nitchras," the name many had for Bob. It literally means "white head" for his blond hair had been bleached white by the sun. But its actual meaning was "one of wisdom," because those with white hair in Ethiopia were oftentimes much older and possessed great wisdom.

Over and over again the girls asked if I must go. "Will you and Mr. Parish not stay with us longer?" "Don't you love us anymore?" "How can you think of leaving us?" Our time together was very heart-wrenching. We cried as we hugged. Then, the new president of the club, Zuriashwork came to me and said the girls had raised some money for a present for me. She handed me a small package wrapped in a tiny piece of cloth. I opened it up to find a beautiful pair of star-shaped golden earrings. At that time I did not have pierced ears, but I told them I would have my ears pierced just so I could wear their lovely gift, and every time I wore them I would think of the many times we were together, the songs we sang, our Christmas play, the cookies we baked for sales, the frustration we had with making our uniforms, the hikes we took, the movie on menstruation, their lessons to me in Amharic, my lessons to them in English, the sad story of Lakech. With each of the memories mentioned, there would be laughter, a sigh, or sorrowful comments.

"You all made my time in Ethiopia so special. You taught me more than I can ever adequately explain to you. I will long reminisce on this country of 'thirteen months of sunshine.' And when I think of your country in the future, I will see your beautiful faces before me."

With many mixed emotions, we left Dessie three days later. People lined the streets to wave farewell and, with tears coursing down my checks, I waved until we went over the rise that blocked the town from view. I sobbed into Bob's shoulder as he tried to console me. I wondered if I would ever see again any of the many people I had grown to know, enjoy and love.

The many mountain passes and heights took us farther and farther from the place I had lovingly called home for two years of my life.

Ahead of me awaited a civil ceremony in Addis and a church wedding in Rome. A new life as a wife loomed before me. And a whole new adventure with the man I loved, whom God brought to me on the other side of the world, was about to begin.

EPILOGUE
WE RETURN TO ETHIOPIA
FORTY YEARS LATER IN 2004

Over the decades we had periodically remained in touch with various Ethiopian friends. There was some difficulty in doing this during the Communist Coup and the devastating drought. We knew that Kebede had remarried and had five more children. Because of military regimes, the last we had heard about him was that he had been imprisoned. We had also heard that Frehiwot had gone through school and become a physician.

Throughout our teaching career in Long Beach, California schools, we had spent many vacations doing volunteer work various places at home and abroad. After retirement, we thought all volunteer work would be halted when Bob was diagnosed with colorectal cancer. He was placed on a permanent colostomy which would involve the use of specialized equipment for the rest of his life. After enduring twenty-eight surgeries, chemo and radiation, we decided to attempt a project in Peru with Medical Ministry International (MMI)—taking all his ostomy equipment with him!

This first venture into foreign travel with an ostomy was such a success that we decided to try another undertaking. Plans to return to Peru the summer of 2004 were underway, when we went to an Ostomy Convention where we heard about Friends of Ostomates Worldwide (FOW). We heard that they had just sent ostomy supplies to Ethiopia. We thought how wonderful it would be to accompany those supplies one day. When we returned from the convention in late August, Bob got on-line with MMI and discovered an eye project was

THIRTEEN MONTHS OF SUNSHINE

scheduled in Ethiopia in October—only five weeks away! Immediate e-mails were sent to MMI. On August 31st came a message to "Join us for the first MMI Project to Ethiopia." Unlike the previous MMI trip of fifty plus volunteers, there would be only five of us, *including* Bob and me! To this historical mountainous country, split in half by the Great Rift Valley, which forms numerous Grand Canyons and high plateaus of 7000-12,000 feet, Bob and I returned October 2004, forty years after being married in the capital of Addis Abeba, at the end of our two years of Peace Corps teaching.

Needless-to-say, a hectic five weeks ensued before the journey. The MMI Eye Clinic was only two weeks. We knew we would need to stay in Ethiopia about a month in order to seek out the Fistula Hospital in Addis and check on the arrival of and additional need for ostomy supplies. We also wanted to search for friends and former students. How were we going to pay for the trip? How does one pack for a month spent on the other side of the world, especially since MMI was sending us tubs and tubs of medical supplies to carry, in addition to our belongings!. There were shots, visas, ostomy supplies to obtain for a month. Who would care for our Dalmatian? We needed to establish contact with FOW (Friends of Ostomates Worldwide) and obtain information on the hospitals and/or other recipients of ostomy supplies in Ethiopia. We had heard that many of our former students and acquaintances had been killed or put into prison during the Communist take-over. Could we possible find any of them still alive?

What an amazing God we have! Pieces of this complex arrangement kept falling into place. Bob's Idyllwild Rotary Club, our Idyllwild Community Presbyterian Church, and individuals supported us financially and with prayers. On-line communication with Fred Moore and Joan Loyd, at FOW, put us in touch with the Women's Fistula Hospital and the Black Lion Hospital in Addis. We had recently been in touch with one of Bob's former Ethiopian students who now lived in Pomona, California, Belay Gabre! {Belay's life story was the subject for a whole book in itself.} He gave us the names of some of his friends in Addis along with phone numbers for them. One of Pat's former students offered to care for our dog, So much just fell into place, and we were OFF TO ETHIOPIA!

We completed the two week Eye Clinic in Soddo, a town one hundred and twenty miles to the south of Addis, where we assisted with 100 cataract surgeries and distributed 1000 reading glasses, We also visited the prison there and asked if anyone knew a man by the name of Kebede Yimam, who had been arrested and placed into prison at least ten years ago because he had worked in the Ministry of Education under the previous regime. We also described his daughter, Frehiwot, who was now a physician. Several said that Kebede had been there, but was there no more.

We returned to the capital and proceeded to contact the Women's Fistula Hospital. After three phone calls to Ruth C. Kennedy, the Liaison Coordinator for the Hospital, we were contacted by Ruth Gadissa. Ruth came to the SIM Guesthouse where we were staying in Addis. This beautiful, thirty year old nurse, who had only two days of stomatherapy training in South Africa, was one of the few nurses in the country trained to work with stomas. Her job was an overwhelming task with hundreds of urostomates. Was she daunted? Not the least! Her lovely smile beamed with joy that God was able to use her in this special way with the thousands of girls who were forced to go through fistula surgery, and the hundreds who resulted in urostomies, due to childbirth.

Her first good news was that the pallet from FOW had arrived, with no problems from Customs, just a few weeks before our arrival! Her second good news was that everything could be used, however NOT at the Fistula Hospital. She had many things taken over to the Black Lion Hospital for their use. Ninety percent of the patients at the Fistula Hospital were urostomates!

What is a fistula? It is an opening or tear in an inner organ, causing leakage, infections and even death. It most commonly occurs during prolonged labor in childbirth. In Ethiopia, it is the custom for girls to marry between twelve and fourteen, or before a first menstrual period. Thus, these young teenagers are frequently giving birth before their own pelvises have fully formed. The fetus is often much too big for an ordinary delivery. Girls are taught to squat and push the baby out. However, after two, three, and four days of excruciating pain in squatting and pushing, the baby is not only dead, but the mother's bladder has ruptured in numerous places. Sometimes the dead fetus is naturally expelled. However, the young wife's problems are just about to begin. Now urine seeps into the vaginal area, and her husband is appalled and leaves her. She has no control over the leakage which can even include fecal matter. She smells horrendous. Her own family may no longer want her. If she doesn't die from infection, she dies from neglect. The fortunate few have family members who will put her on a pallet and carry her the three, four or more days' walk up and down mountain pathways to get her to a hospital that hopefully can perform the correct surgery to mend the young girl. This goes on daily in thousands of grass huts throughout Ethiopia. There are projects going on to encourage later marriage for women, but customs held to for thousands of years are difficult to change.

Ruth Gadissa gave us a list of the urostomy materials needed, which we have passed on to the FOW Warehouse and Joan Loyd, Ruth also requested booklets that would show pictures of people wearing or putting on flanges and bags. Any video of such procedures would also be welcome since they do have VHS access. Ruth profusely told us to thank FOW for all the crèmes, ointments, powders, and belts. These girls were very small in size. Remember, most of them were thirteen to sixteen years old. Miss Gadissa helped them to measure their stomas with the use of templates that we had with us.

She gave us a "shopping list" of supplies needed. With her excellent English, she was apologetic for requesting so much, but emphasized how none of these supplies are available anywhere in the country.

We asked her if she had heard of a Dr. Frehiwot Kebede,. She said she would make inquiries. We also asked many at the SIM guesthouse, where we were staying in Addis, if they knew of a Dr. Frehiwot Kebede. They also said they would make inquiries.

Seeing our old town of Dessie was one of our objectives. Friends we made in Soddo arranged a flight for us to Cambolsha which had a landing strip that was near the town where we had taught. In Cambolsha we were picked up by Pastor Alabachew Teshoma who met us at the little airport and drove us up the mountain to Dessie. We were provided with a guesthouse on the Mekane Yesus compound. Alabachew drove us to all the places we remembered. All three of the houses where I had lived were still standing. Bob's house, however, had blown up from ammunition stored in it during one of the coups. The piazza now had a number of buildings with several stories. The old Telecommunications Building was still there as was our school. We went up to visit the place where we had spent so much time. The headmaster took us on a tour of the compound. We were delighted to find one of Bob's former Ethiopian students now teaching there, Wobetu Gabre. When we saw him, he recognized Bob immediately as Mr. Parish. When I asked him if he remembered me, he thought for a moment, muttered Tsahainesh, and then called me Miss Summers. I was amazed that after forty years he could recall my maiden name! He certainly had a remarkable memory. We all walked around the compound and reminisced. Much was the same. The main difference was a large outhouse that had been constructed on the compound.

We also visited the Dessie Regional Hospital and have since sent medical supplies there through FOW.

Upon our return to Addis, there was a message for us from one of the clinics in town. I called the number. After a long pause, a lovely throaty voice answered and I asked if a Dr. Frehiwot Kebede worked there. There was another long pause. The same voice asked, "Is this Miss Summers, the one called 'Tsahainesh?' The teacher of my mother Lakech Ali? You married Mr. Parish and are now called Mrs. Parish?" the throaty voice continued to ask in impeccable English.

"Yes!" I excitedly replied. "I am now called Mrs. Parish. And do I have the daughter of Lakech Ali and Kebede Yimam? The daughter called Frehiwot?"

"Oh yes," she replied. She continued to inquire of my health and Bob's health. I excitedly responded to her questions and asked her questions about her well being, her husband, and her father, Kebede. She said they were all well and her father was out of prison just these past three months. She said that both she and her husband were doctors. She asked where we were staying and said she would be right there to pick us up and take us to her home. When her taxi entered the compound, a beautiful young woman stepped forth. We looked at each other and then fell into each other's arms weeping. We were both asking if it were really true. Bob stood by smiling. I kept saying how proud her mother would be. She told us to pack our suitcases and come with her to stay in her home. We had to meet her three young daughters, her husband and to see her father, whom I had not seen in forty years. She said we had so much to talk about and she wanted to know everything about her mother.

Fre's home was a beautiful, two-story stone house with three bathrooms. Her handsome husband was so cordial. I looked at Lakech's granddaughters, three beautiful, bright energetic children. Fre was everything for which Lakech had shown promise.

Kebede had remarried and had had five more children. He came over for a short visit. He, like us, had aged. The eleven years, eight months in prison had caused many physical ailments.

It would take at least one more book to tell of our short time with renewed acquaintances in Ethiopia. We have been trying to get Fre's sister, Yetnayet, here to the U.S., but in post 9/11 America we have met one obstacle after another.

Suffice it to say that Ethiopia continues to be our second home where loving and adored family members abound. Perhaps one of Fre's children will come to study in the U.S. one of these years. I know Lakech would be so proud.